Why do normal, intelligent people
   join a cult?
Once they understand what's going
   on, why do they stay?
How could hundreds of people
   willingly commit suicide?
Will it happen again?

Bonnie Thielmann's amazing story demonstrates
the answers to such gnawing questions. It shows
how the prejudices and shortcomings of
mainstream society give rise to dangerous
groups. It also shows the power of divine love to
surround a shattered human being and restore
her to wholeness and balance.

The whole world knows what happened the
dreadful evening of November 18, 1978, in
Jonestown. This is the book that explains why.

# the broken god

BONNIE
THIELMANN
WITH
DEAN MERRILL

David C. Cook Publishing Co.

ELGIN, ILLINOIS—WESTON, ONTARIO

First printing January, 1979
Second printing February, 1979

© 1979 David C. Cook Publishing Co.

Edited by Marshall Shelley
Designed by Kurt Dietsch
Printed in the United States of America

ISBN: 0-89191-180-4
LC: 78-75025

*To my precious son, Stephan;*
*and to one of the few Prince Charmings*
*left in the world,*
*my beloved husband, Hank*

*In memory of*
*Leo Joseph Ryan*

*"Greater love hath no man than this,*
*that a man lay down his life for his friends."*

# CONTENTS

# PREFACE

When a book is written, the author is often asked why. In this book, I have made myself vulnerable to the public eye by relating my intimate story and, with it, my feelings, thoughts, and emotions. I have done so shortly after emerging from a real-life nightmare in Guyana. The closest parallel I can find to writing this book is the way it would feel to pour acid into fresh, deep wounds.

My purposes have been three:

—To answer valid questions about the inside of Peoples Temple. What magnetism drew people into this pseudo-religious organization? Why did it masquerade as a religious group? What kind of thinking allowed the command for mass suicide to be given—and obeyed?

—To help those of us who believe in God to recognize our own shortcomings in actually living out the principles Christ gave us—wherever we are and whatever we do. By recognizing our weaknesses and then strengthening them, I believe we can prevent future Jonestowns.

—To tell the intimate story of my loss of faith and hope, the depths to which I fell, and how God's love and compassion reached me even as I cursed him. I do not pretend to be a model Christian. I have much growing yet to do and am still in the process of sorting out the misconceptions of earlier years and conforming my ideas and values to the Scriptures. Nevertheless, I believe that what God has done in my life is genuine, and I desire to spark faith in the hearts of many who have lost it, never had it, or feel too alienated and far away ever to find God.

My thanks go to my husband, who cared enough for the truth to be published that he gave up his bride of five months for more than a week after I had just returned from Guyana in order that this book could be started.

My thanks go to my parents, whom I put through hell, and yet they loved me through it all.

My gratitude goes to Dean Merrill, who spent hours away from his family to interview me and then write the manuscript; to his wife, Grace, who, true to her name, graciously gave up her husband, caring alone for three children under the age of six despite a broken foot. During those days she also coped with a case of pneumonia in one of their three-year-old twins.

Finally, but not least, I send my appreciation to Sisters Anne Fletcher and Margaret Burns, who protected me at the Cenacle Retreat House in Warrenville, Illinois, where the interviews for this book took place. They provided a peaceful atmosphere, and their loving concern for my emotional turmoil was very touching. They were a perfect example of Christ's love breaking down all barriers; we are all God's children.

# one GEORGETOWN

THE PAN AMERICAN 707 droned on through the night as I peered into the moonlight for a glimpse of the Guyana coast. All around me sat the two dozen or so members of the Leo Ryan delegation—the congressman and his aides, reporters and photographers, and thirteen desperate relatives—some of them making this trip for the second time—hoping to see their loved ones in the settlement somewhere below called Jonestown. It was Tuesday night, November 14, 1978.

I was unique among them: I had no blood kin in the Peoples Temple commune. But I had come out of a concern just as deep, a hope that Jim Jones would still listen to his "precious daughter," as he had often called me, and would let me escort out those who wished to leave his jungle kingdom. I knew Marceline, his wife, would put her arms around me once more and welcome me to the household where I had spent some of the most important parts of my life. Even though I had left Peoples Temple a few years earlier, I had kept a good relationship with the Joneses ever since, and Marceline had often slipped away to my house for rest and rejuvenation. If I could only see them again, perhaps the fears of those around me on the plane could be laid to rest.

It was 11:30 P.M. when we finally settled onto the tarmac of Temehri Airport at Georgetown, Guyana's capital. Jonestown lay 150 jungle miles to the northwest. The oppressive tropical heat and humidity came steaming toward our faces as the aircraft door was opened. The congressman, a fatherly 53-year-old with silver hair and a lean frame, was whisked off to receive the hospitality of American ambassador John Burke, while the rest of us on the crowded flight formed long lines at the customs checkpoint and waited to explain why we had come to this obscure corner of South America.

Thus it was not until the next day that Leo Ryan and I were able to continue the conversation we had briefly begun during a stopover in Port-of-Spain, Trinidad. At that time we had barely touched the basic facts—that I had lived with the Joneses as a teenager in Brazil, that they had considered me one of the family, that I had named my two children after two of theirs, and that I knew the movement from inside out—before it was time to reboard. Sitting now in the lobby of Georgetown's Pegasus Hotel, we resumed our discussion, and I explained how much the Joneses still meant to me.

"You know," he said after a while, "I think it would be really good if you came with me to the ambassador's house tonight for dinner. I think your story would carry a lot of weight with him."

Leo decided to take one of the concerned relatives as well, a bearded, six-foot-six young black man named Jim Cobb, whose mother, brothers, and thirteen-year-old sister lived in Jonestown. The two of us went with Leo at six o'clock that evening a half block down the street to the ambassador's plantation-style mansion. We sat talking in the large receiving room until Mr. Burke finally appeared, and in spite of Leo's polite introductions, it became obvious that the ambassador did not wish to add two more plates to his table. Jim Cobb and I eased ourselves out of the situation and returned to the hotel.

I was convinced, anyway, that my best chances for success at Jonestown lay in keeping my distance from the Ryan group. Peoples Temple had little reason to appreciate the coming of a congressman or his band of complaining relatives. I had to make my appeal directly to Jim Jones, and I had to do it with total innocence. When Leo appeared at the hotel later that evening, I told him "Tomorrow morning I'm going to go out to Lamaha Gardens" (the Peoples Temple headquarters in Georgetown) "and make arrangements to see Jim and Marcie."

"Bonnie," he said, "that's not safe. I was already there this morning, and it's not exactly a friendly place."

"No, Leo—I have to go alone. I can't be connected with anybody else. All I'm going to do is come in like old times and say, 'Hi, everybody—I've been hearing the news, and I was concerned about all of you, and I want to see Jim.' "

We got into an argument about whether I should be allowed to do that. Finally Leo said, "All right—I'll let you go, on one condition: you must go upstairs and write a letter to both John Burke and myself, promising that if you're successful and you actually get permission to go, you'll be back from Jonestown within twenty-four hours of your departure. And if you're not, we are authorized to come get you."

"You've got a deal."

But when I came downstairs Thursday morning with my letter, he reneged.

"I don't want you to go out there, Bonnie. It's just too dangerous."

"Leo—I thought we discussed all that last night," I said with a tinge of irritation.

"My God, you're a stubborn woman!" he exclaimed, and we both broke into laughter.

We finally agreed, after further dickering, that I could have one hour at Lamaha Gardens to try to make arrangements, and that Leo's driver provided by the embassy would take me and wait for me while I was inside. By mid-morning I was on my way out to the edge of the city to the large two-story building surrounded by a wrought-iron fence.

My heart began pounding. I knew I simply had to play this casual, or I might never get any cooperation from Linda Sharon Amos, the person in charge of Lamaha Gardens. We had known each other back in California since 1971, and I had adored her children, especially Martin, who was now a brilliant nine-year-old. But Linda had been watching from the door of the airport customs area when we arrived, checking to see who had come, and I feared that I might be guilty by association.

The gate was standing open, and so I prepared to make my entrance. I jammed my clammy hands into my jeans pockets and began sauntering toward the building when suddenly Linda came storming out the front door.

"Get off this property! This is private property! Get off, or I'm calling the police!"

By this time, I was close enough to reach out and touch

her as I pulled off my sunglasses. Perhaps she had not recognized me. "Linda, it's me—Bonnie," I answered.

"Oh" was all she said for a moment. The fear suddenly drained out of me, and I relaxed.

But she soon resumed her belligerence. "I know who you are—and you came with the enemies," she snapped.

"Yes, Linda, I came on the same plane, and I'm even rooming with one of the mothers who wants to see her son. But I want you to know that I came down because I'm Jim and Marcie's daughter, and I'm concerned. I'm not your enemy. All I want to do is see Marcie. . . ."

She was adamant. "Get off this property before I call the police."

I pressed my point. "Listen, Linda—I have letters right here in my purse in Jim's own handwriting telling me that I'm welcome to visit them anytime I choose. And I choose now."

She began edging me toward the gate. "You sure picked a bad time to visit, with all the enemies. If you have anything to say to me, use the phone and make an appointment."

"No, Linda, I'm not going to call you on the phone and tell you what I just told you face to face. Now you just get on the ham radio to Jonestown and tell Jim I'm here and want to see him."

Finally she relented. "Okay—I'll tell him what you said." By this time she had closed the gate and nudged me out onto the sidewalk.

I gave her my room number at the Pegasus Hotel and asked if she would promise to let me know Jim's response.

"I'm not promising anything."

And then, all of a sudden, something happened that was entirely unplanned. I reached my hand through the gate and gently laid it on her arm as I said, "Linda . . . I

**15**

love you. I'm here because I really care. This hasn't been any fun trip for me; I came because I'm concerned about you." I started to cry.

And this tough, hardbitten woman, who claimed to have been a member of the Charles Manson gang at one time, began to cry, too. She tried to choke back the tears, but they came anyway.

"Well, all I know is that you're here with a group of people who are out to destroy us," she repeated, but underneath I knew that a soft spot had been touched in both of us.

I didn't get an answer until late the next day, on Friday after Leo Ryan and the group had left for Jonestown. I was disappointed not to be able to accompany them, but the Guyana Airways plane Leo had chartered held only nineteen people, and since he had put up most of the money, it was his to decide who went and who stayed. He decided it was more important to have the media along, so only four seats were left for relatives. The rest could always come later if things went well. The relatives had no choice but to sit down on Friday morning and take a vote to select who would get to go. The vote went to Jim Cobb, who had been one of Jim's bodyguards; Anthony Katsaris, brother of Jim's assistant Maria Katsaris; Beverly Oliver; and Carol Boyd. Jim and Beverly were black, Anthony and Carol were white. It seemed a good representation.

Their departure for the airport at two o'clock that afternoon was a fearful time for all of us. Leo was wearing a red and blue striped polo shirt, and I slipped my arm around his waist there in front of the hotel as I said, "Leo, promise me you won't spend the night in Jonestown." Now the tables were turned, and I was pleading with him to be cautious. "You don't know how Jim Jones' mind works. There's nothing he won't do to stop you. I know you're getting a late start in the day, but if you stay overnight, he could send some naked woman into your room and then flash the picture all across the States—he'll do anything."

He squeezed me back, kissed me on the cheek, and said, "Honey, you don't know me. I'd like to see him try it."

I urged him to give Marceline Jones the same message I had given Linda Amos—that I was in Georgetown and was hoping for a way to come see them. And with that, Leo was gone.

It was late that evening when my roommate returned from a trip of her own out to Lamaha Gardens with the good news that both she and I had been cleared to come to Jonestown. She had talked with her son by radio, and Linda Amos had said she could go to see him in person. Then Linda had added, "Oh, yes—tell Bonnie that I talked to Father this afternoon, and he said to tell her to come ahead."

I was ecstatic. We began making plans to pack up early the next morning and be ready to go when the chartered plane made its return run to pick up Leo and the rest. My fears for their safety overnight were forgotten in the anticipation that, after three full days in the country, I would finally get to Jonestown.

Saturday, November 18, dawned hot and sticky as usual. I was packing my sleeping bag and other items for being in the jungle when the telephone rang. It was Jim Schollert, the congressman's aide, calling from Lamaha Gardens, where he had just received a one-sentence radio message from Leo:

"Tell Bonnie she can't use my plane."

It was against all precedent. Leo had been nothing but cordial to me the entire week, eager to hear about my past with the Joneses, and hopeful that I could do some good

17

once I saw them again. He wasn't a capricious sort of man; I could only conclude that things were not going well in Jonestown, and that Leo was laying a very serious message between the lines.

My roommate and I vented our disappointment to each other and toyed with the idea of disobeying him and boarding the outbound plane anyway. Jim Jones' invitation still stood; he had welcomed me the same as in years gone by. But something was definitely wrong.

She and I decided to stop and pray together for direction. By the time we finished, we both knew we must not go until we found out more. There was nothing to do but wait . . . and remember.

1-18-80

DEAR JONATHAN, MARY JEAN,
JOY & JAMIE:

I was glad you had a
good quality time with
Wil, Rita, Michael, Robbie
& John Mark over the holidays
We are looking forward
to a good year ahead.

I trust you all will enjoy
the book.

Cassette tapes will be
available in Feb. for
$6.00 ea.

I enjoyed talking with you
after such a long time.

If you could send $3.95 plus
postage it would help. Thanks.

Love Hank, Bonnie & Steve

Hank & Bonnie Shellmann
123 Tree Frog Ln.
Santa Cruz Ca. 95060
405 426-1926

# TWO THE RAINBOW FAMILY

IT WAS EARLY IN 1962, and my father was waiting in line at the Belo Horizonte post office when a clerk motioned him over to his window.

"You're an American," he said. "Can you translate for this man?" My father looked into the face of a handsome, black-haired man about thirty years old with a package in his hand.

"Sure—how can I help you?" my father asked. Once the package was processed and paid for, he introduced himself as the two walked out into the Brazilian sunshine.

"I'm Ed Malmin—a missionary here for the last three years. Did you just come to Belo?"

"Yes, just recently," the man replied. "My name's Jim

Jones, and we're from Indianapolis. My family and I are
still living in a hotel until we find a place."

Within a few minutes my father had learned that he
was a pastor of a growing church called Peoples Temple,
but that he had left the congregation in the hands of
associates in order to come to Brazil. He sounded as if he
intended to stay for a while, although he didn't say what
for.

It was only natural that my father invite the Joneses to
our home in the suburb of Venda Nova for a meal during
those first days of adjustment to a new country. To sit
around a table with North Americans and speak English
together would be a welcome treat. The date was set.

Jim Jones told me later that something sparked between the two of them that day at the post office. Ed
Malmin impressed him almost immediately as a person
of integrity, a man to be trusted. He had found a friend,
but even more than that, a seasoned colleague to whom
he could turn with the questions he carried inside.

My parents and my brother, Mark, were glad to entertain the newcomers; the only person who scowled about it
was me. At the age of sixteen, I thought of myself as more
Brazilian than American. I had lived in this country all of
my teen years; I loved its people, and I smoldered inside
at the condescending attitudes of the American missionaries I knew toward the Brazilians. I could see no
reason why my Nordic features were in any way superior
to the darkened complexions around me on the streets
each day. The matter was more than just academic: it had
become a personal issue because of my Brazilian boyfriend, a dark-haired, dark-eyed engineering student
whom I had been dating for almost a year. I loved him; in
fact, we were unofficially engaged. Many of my friends in
Brazil were already married by this age, and I had no
reason to wait any longer.

To the missionaries, it was scandalous.

And now more Americans were coming. I stayed in my room that evening as long as I could, opening the door only when my mother announced that the meal was ready. I immediately recognized Marceline Jones as the woman I had seen a day or two before in the Belo Horizonte shopping district—and had crossed to the opposite sidewalk to avoid. Her blond hair piled high on her head marked her immediately as an American, and the fewer of those I encountered, the better.

But the children—what was this? Only one was Caucasian, a three-year-old named Stephan. Two of the others were oriental—a girl who appeared to be about eight, and a boy named Lou just a bit older than Stephan. The toddler, Jimmy, was undeniably black.

They were all cheerfully introduced by their parents, with a comment about "our rainbow family." My mind was spinning as we gathered around the table. These people obviously did not share the racial prejudices I had expected.

The dinner conversation eventually came around to me and what I was doing—that I had recently finished high school by correspondence study through the American School, a Chicago-based program; that I was working now as a secretary-interpreter for an aged missionary named Nellie Murdock and making good money, as good as some Brazilian men with families; that I would probably return to the States in the fall for college. One other fact came out under questioning: my boyfriend. I held my breath to await the reaction.

There was none. Jim and Marceline Jones went right on eating without a remark, a raising of the eyes, or even a pause. I picked up my fork again, and soon the talk had moved to safer topics.

Jim explained that they had come to our city to rest

from the pressures of their ministry in the States. He also spoke in earnest tones about how important it was to find a place to hide from the nuclear holocaust that was sure to come. At any time, some nervous politician might press the button that would launch World War III, and the whole world would be engulfed in radioactive fallout.

He had read an article in *Esquire* magazine the year before listing the nine safest places to be in the event of nuclear war. One of them was Eureka, California. Another was Belo Horizonte, Brazil, and so he had come with his family to see if this might be a haven to which his entire congregation should migrate. It simply wasn't safe to stay in the United States any longer, he said, not only because of the threat of war but also because of racial bigotry.

They told of the pain of losing Stephany, a Korean war orphan they had adopted, who had been killed in a car accident with four other church members—and how no white undertaker in Indianapolis would bury her. Jim was certain that such a society was doomed to destruction.

My reluctance was gone. Here was indeed a sincere and honest Christian couple who practiced what all the rest preached. I didn't know a lot about the danger of bombs and missiles, but I knew how I felt about their openness and acceptance. At last I had found some Americans whom I could respect, and I wanted to help them in any way I could.

The opportunity came soon. In the days that followed, I found myself spending almost more time with the Joneses than with my own family, translating for them and helping them get settled. I would take the children from the hotel to the huge park directly across from the Belo Horizonte post office where my father and Jim had first met. For a few hours I would tenderly mother this wonderful assortment of children. Even Brazilians in the park would stare at me as I cuddled little Jimmy with his kinky black hair, and they couldn't resist asking, "Is that baby yours?"

The Joneses eventually found a very simple three-bedroom house with a veranda, and it was soon agreed that I might as well move in with them for the months that remained until September. I was ecstatic. The typical teenage skirmishes with my parents about how I dressed and where I went, and especially about my boyfriend, were all in the past.

It was a simple home, without rugs on the floor or a washing machine to keep up with the needs of young children. The three boys had a bedroom together; the daughter and I shared a bedroom; and Jim and Marcie had the third. There were no bedspreads; each bed had only a pair of sheets and a single blanket. The only income came from the church back in Indianapolis; as a result, our usual diet was bread and rice, sometimes with beans or another vegetable. Meat was the exception.

Nevertheless, it was a happy place. Jim regaled the parrot each new day with "I love Polly in the morning . . ." to the tune of "I Love Paris in the Springtime." Marceline would bathe the three young boys at one time in the bathtub, and stand back to admire the beauty of the black, oriental, and white bodies all splashing together. The toilet training of little Jimmy was a family affair. Every time he was successful, we would all crowd into the little bathroom to clap and cheer, even his father.

Jim and Marcie were constantly reinforcing to the adopted children that they had been specially chosen to be a part of this family, and Stephan, the only biological child in the house, began to show signs of tension at one point. When Marcie realized what was happening, she took him in her arms and assured him that he was indeed their son. She got out snapshots of Stephan nursing as a baby in order to make the point that he belonged to them as securely as any of the others.

Stephan was always, however, the most fiercely determined of the lot. One day when Marceline had a bit of extra money, she and I went to the butcher shop two blocks away, leaving the children with Maria, a fourteen-year-old Brazilian girl who did housework for us. Stephan was determined to come along.

"No, you can't go, Stephan," his mother said. "You must stay here with Maria, and we'll be back in a little while."

We were standing in line at the butcher shop when all of a sudden a small boy touched our legs.

"What are you doing here? How did you get out of the house?" we exclaimed.

A mischievous smile crossed his face. "I hit Maria with a broom."

Back at the house, we learned that he was not exaggerating. He wanted to go to the butcher shop, and when Maria wouldn't let him go, he gave her a good whack with the broom in order to escape. Maria was in tears, but Marceline said, "Under the circumstances, you don't need to feel badly. I guess he really did want to go!"

Jim showed his tenderness as well when someone, out of concern for our meager diet, gave us a duck to eat. Jim couldn't bring himself to kill it, but kept it instead in the backyard as a pet. It made a terrible mess, and finally we arrived at a solution: we would take the duck to the park across from the post office and turn it loose there to swim on the pond with the others. The only trouble was, the others immediately began to peck at this intruder, and we hurried Jim away from the pond before he could watch the demise of his beloved pet.

The same compassion was showered upon the hungry

Brazilian children on the streets. Whereas the missionaries I had known always locked their houses tight against beggars and said you couldn't start feeding one without being overrun, the Joneses were soon feeding an extra ten to fifteen children every day. Marceline would cook rice in a large five-quart pot, and we would dish their food into bowls and plates at the same time as we served ourselves. We didn't have enough table space for them in addition to the seven of us, so we let them sit by the kitchen door or out on the veranda to eat. Night after night they came, and they were always served the same evening meal we ate. It was probably their only meal of the day.

It was this kind of loving action that established Marceline Jones as my new role model. Up to this point, my secret idol had always been movie star Brigitte Bardot; I had done my best to copy her saucy image. Now I thought to myself, "Here I am always thinking about my appearance and trying to be sexy—and here's Marceline, who seems to have almost no vanity at all. She's content to get up in the morning, pull her hair into a pony tail, and get to work serving her family and other people." I decided right then that inner beauty was going to be my new goal.

One day I came home with Jim to find Marceline's blue eyes clouded from crying. She was never able to conceal her tears very well, and I immediately asked what was the matter.

"Oh, honey," she said quietly, "I'm just facing some things about myself that I haven't wanted to face—some selfishness and some other things that I really want to change."

I couldn't imagine what in the world she was talking about. As for myself, I would be grateful if I could come even close to her standard.

# three AN INDELIBLE MARK

I WASN'T THE ONLY PERSON to be favorably impressed by the Joneses. A Belo Horizonte newspaper eventually did a large feature story about this unique family from North America who could have had children of their own, but chose to stop after one—Stephan—and adopt needy children of various races instead.

From time to time Jim met with government officials, learning as much as he could about the country and its systems, trying to determine whether this would be a safe haven from the imminent nuclear horror. He spent his days reading and thinking, often sitting crosslegged on the bare floor of the living room poring over the newspaper and calling me to translate: "Bonnie—tell me what this says. What does this headline say? Read this article to me."

He was most attentive, of course, to anything about military hardware. Anytime we were out in the city and saw any large pointed shape—even a church steeple—he would begin to rave about missiles. "They don't know what they're doing," he would say. "They don't know what's going to come." I was a naive sixteen-year-old, of course, so I dismissed it as one of his idiosyncracies. Even when he showed me a picture of him and Marceline standing on either side of Fidel Castro, whom they had met during a Cuban stopover en route to Brazil, I wasn't particularly alarmed.

I was more impressed with his fears that something would happen to me personally. He worried about my being kidnapped and demonstrated for me where to stick my knee if I were ever attacked by a man. Although he and Marceline liked my Brazilian boyfriend—I have warm memories of he and I coming in after a date and sitting on the edge of their twin beds to tell them about the movie we'd seen or where we'd been—Jim was still concerned that I might get pregnant. My boyfriend was typically Latin, and after he had licked my neck in front of the Joneses, Jim had a fatherly chat with me.

"I can tell he's really aggressive, Bonnie. I see him touching you all the time—you've got to be careful."

"Jim," I answered, "you really don't need to worry so much. I promise you nothing's going to happen."

Nevertheless, Jim provided me with a male contraceptive to carry in my purse just in case. "I believe you," he said, "but please promise me that you'll carry this in your purse wherever you go."

I took it—and thought to myself how much fun it would be to give it back to Jim when my parents shipped me back to the States. I could hardly wait for the opportunity to show him how virtuous I'd been.

It was a genuine tragedy sometime later when I lost my purse. I was heartbroken. I could replace the perfume and the money and the ID and the photos, but what bothered me most was that I'd never have the joy of returning the condom unopened.

Jim also complained at times about the lurid posters and marquees of the Brazilian cinemas, especially, as he always put it, "those women with their breasts hanging out." After a few mentions, it became apparent that he had a definite aversion to buxom women. He later told a story about being interviewed by a shapely reporter who tried to seduce him. She allegedly exposed herself and made the comment "Aren't they beautiful?" Jim claimed to have found it all very disgusting. Whether the story was true or apocryphal I don't know; it is a fact, however, that in later years many of his mistresses were small-chested.

I assumed, of course, that the source of his morality was his Christian conviction. But the evidence was lacking. For example, the Bible was absent from the Jones home, in spite of his being a pastor. I had no way of knowing that even before leaving Indiana he had begun to denounce the Virgin Birth from his pulpit and had once thrown a Bible to the floor with the complaint, "Too many people are looking at this instead of me." He had also made a pilgrimage to Philadelphia in the late 1950s for a private audience with Father Divine, the black cult leader, and when he returned, he began to make greater and greater demands of loyalty from his people.

Prayer was a missing item as well. When I first came to live with the Joneses, I noticed that they omitted the mealtime grace, and so I asked if I could lead in prayer before eating. From then on, I was the official pray-er at the table.

One day a crisis arose when it looked as if Jim might have to return to the States. Both he and Marceline were upset, and I wanted to reach out to them and do something to quiet their fears. Impulsively I said, "Listen—give me your hands, and let's pray together." The three of us stood in a circle in the living room holding hands as I prayed fervently for God to intervene. They both were appreciative, but did not volunteer to pray in their own behalf.

We all went to my father's church each Sunday and to the midweek service as well. But Jim was never called upon to preach. Perhaps that was because of what my father was hearing in his private counseling sessions with Jim. The two spent a great deal of time together. Jim wanted to know what my father believed about the blood of Christ: was it really to be considered an atonement for sin?

Secondly, he was not at all sure about the Trinity. Apparently my father made little headway with him on this subject, because shortly after Jim's return to Indianapolis in 1964, he would make jokes such as "I don't know whether there's one God or eighteen."

Finally, he wanted to know whether my father believed in such things as demons. But when confronted with Scripture as well as the voice of experience on this subject, Jim would brush it all aside and become quarrelsome. My father eventually became frustrated with a man who seemed to drink the water offered to him and then spit it back out again.

Strangely enough, however, Jim was deeply attracted to my father's Bible. He constantly wanted to hold it. "I feel such power when your Bible is in my hands," he said. "I feel a new surge of strength every time I hold it."

At one point Jim asked him to accompany him to a Brazilian spiritist meeting. "How can I do that?" my

29

father asked. "How can I move from light back into darkness? It would be a denial of all that I know to be the truth." Jim became very angry and went to the meeting alone, and continued to investigate Brazil's various cults.

All of this was of course beyond my center of interest as a teenager. Only a few of his doubts were transplanted to my mind, such as how there could be so much misery and suffering in the world if God were such a benevolent Father. I didn't know how to answer that, and I was afraid to ask anyone; instead, I buried the question in my subconscious. Inside of me, I was afraid that other Christians might not know the answers either, and if they didn't, my whole set of beliefs would come tumbling down. So it was safer not to raise the questions.

I had little time to worry about theology, anyway, because a more immediate storm was brewing: the time was quickly coming when I would have to leave these wonderful people and enroll at Bethany Fellowship Missionary Training Center in frigid, faraway Minneapolis. I could not think of a single reason for going. It would mean leaving the Joneses. It would mean leaving my boyfriend. And it would mean leaving warm, multiracial Brazil for the cold, bigoted United States. Jim and Marceline stayed out of the running argument with my parents on this subject, even though they felt Bible school would prove to be useless.

On my own, I tried to get help from a young Brazilian banker I knew who had a large ranch. We laid a few plans for me to be hidden on his ranch until I reached age eighteen and could chart my own course. But soon he thought better of it and decided he didn't want to risk a jail term by harboring an American minor.

I was trapped. My depression grew from day to day; my seventeenth birthday came and went in August without making any permanent mark in my memory; I could only think about the approaching exile. In my immaturity, death seemed better than any of the other options. I began making my plans for suicide. It was in some ways a typical teen snap decision, but the crisis was both real and urgent in my mind, and I had to do something.

On a Sunday afternoon, after the midday meal at my parents' house, I left alone on the city bus for a large lake called Pampulha. It was a beautiful site, ringed by palm trees, with a long concrete pier extending out to a dam where the water plunged down to a lower level. At the end of the pier was a cul-de-sac no more than twelve feet in diameter, with a four-foot railing around the edge.

The bus pulled to the edge of the main artery that ran alongside Pampulha, and I got off. I carefully checked to make sure that no one else was in the area. No swimming was allowed here because of parasites in the water, and there was no place for parking. I studied the row of palm trees and concluded that they were too thin to conceal anyone. Then I crawled over the gate and began to walk out on the block-long pier.

I kept thinking how much I loved Brazil and my boyfriend, and how I would rather be dead in Brazil than alive in the United States. When I reached the cul-de-sac, I carefully deposited my purse, sunglasses, and a couple of books on the railing, which was about a foot wide. I wanted to be kind to my parents by leaving them an unmistakable clue, so they would know I hadn't been kidnapped or raped instead.

I turned once more to check the way I had just come to make sure no one was watching. The palm trees stood silently while the traffic continued to whirr past. The grassy fringe below the palm trees was empty, as was the pier itself. I was indeed alone, and the time had come to carry out the last act of my life.

I turned to face the churning water. I took one deep

breath and then jumped up to get one knee onto the top of the railing. Quickly I brought the other knee up, stopped a moment to steady myself, and then planted one foot on the railing ledge in order to stand upright.

I could not get up. Something was clutching at the back of my blouse, holding me back. I whirled around to look into the face of a man who had appeared out of nowhere. He had a mustache, and he wore the simple straw-and-canvas shoes of the poor people of Brazil. The expression in his dark eyes was neither anxious nor condemning; he just stood there holding onto my blouse.

My mind was screaming inside, *Where could he have come from? I checked everywhere; there was no one in sight and no place to hide!* It was a physical impossibility for him to have jumped the gate and run the length of the pier in the few seconds between my last check and the time he grabbed me. But there he stood. He said not a word, and so the only thing for me to do was to crawl back down onto the concrete.

I felt a tremendous wave of humiliation, and tried for a moment to pretend that I had simply wanted to look at the scenery. It wouldn't work. He kept staring at me in silence. I tried to dodge his look; I waited for him to walk away or say something. He would do neither; his only action was to keep looking at me. Finally I picked up my purse and other things and moved back toward the shore, leaving him still standing there. To this day I don't know who he was or how he got there.

I was too ashamed to tell either my parents or the Joneses about what had happened. I simply hung on through the final days of packing, suffering inside the pain of the inevitable. When the day of departure arrived, I was disappointed that neither Jim nor Marceline came to the airport; instead, I was stuck with a bunch of missionaries for whom I cared little, singing a mournful stanza of "God Be With You Till We Meet Again."

I was not to see the Joneses for eight years, and yet their influence never left me. The memories of Marceline cooking and dancing the Charleston at the same time in her kitchen to the music of a tinny transistor radio . . . of her running down to the bus stop in a downpour to meet Jim with a big black umbrella so he wouldn't be drenched . . . of going with her to the hairdresser and coming home to hear Jim say, "Wow, you two really look beautiful"—they were indelibly etched in my mind, and I could only hope that my own adult years would be so joyous.

# four ANOTHER STEPHAN, ANOTHER STEPHANY

BY THE END OF MY SECOND year of Bible school, I was engaged to a tall, dark-haired student from New York. My father performed our wedding ceremony that July in our family's home church in Chicago, and at the age of not-quite-nineteen I became Mrs. Bonnie Burnham. One more year of study followed, and then came our year of internship in the pastorate of a small rural church in western New York.

Meanwhile, Jim and Marceline had moved from Belo Horizonte to Rio de Janeiro, where Jim put the family on a firmer financial base by teaching at the American school. He had earned a bachelor's degree in education from Butler University while struggling in his early days to establish himself as a pastor. My parents kept in touch, and when it came time for their furlough, Jim wondered whether my father would be open to going to Peoples Temple in Indianapolis on a short-term basis. The denominational executives approved, and so my parents found themselves in the Midwest for six to eight months.

During that time, my father of course preached a solidly evangelical Christianity, which was a bit different from what the congregation was used to hearing. He left the church sometime in 1964 when Jim returned, having decided that the Brazilian government was not stable enough and that he would have to seek elsewhere for a refuge. My parents relocated in southern California for the rest of their furlough.

They were back in Brazil for a second term of missionary service when my husband and I arrived in late 1966 to work with orphan children under Bethany Fellowship. Not only was I excited to be back in the warm country I loved, but my return signaled a special passage for me personally on another score. My husband and I had prayed for divine guidance on when to start a family, and we had separately come to the same conclusion that we should wait until we had landed in Brazil.

I didn't totally understand why, especially when so many of my college friends were already new mothers. Deep within me I wanted a child; I wanted to provide the kind of love and care I had seen Marceline Jones give so selflessly.

So the very first night after our arrival in Rio, I lay in the darkness of my parents' second-floor apartment praying, "OK, God—now? I've waited two and a half years to get to this moment; is this the right time? If so, please show me in a supernatural way."

The next morning after breakfast, my mother took me

into a spare bedroom and began to display all the clothes she had been making for a granddaughter. She excitedly pulled out dainty sleepers and darling little dresses as she dropped rather obvious hints with a twinkle in her eye.

I admired her handiwork with oohs and ahhs, but inside I was praying, *God . . . this really isn't enough of a sign. She would have showed me all these things whether I had prayed last night or not.* At almost that exact moment we heard my father shout from the veranda overlooking the cobblestone street. It was an intense scream, with such fright in his voice that I instantly thought he had suffered a heart attack. We both came running.

"Look! Look in the street!" he shouted. He was standing with his arm stretched toward the street below, and was obviously not having a heart attack.

We stared into the street. We saw nothing unusual.

"What are you talking about?" I cried.

He had a perplexed look on his face, and finally he said, "I was out here just reading my Bible and meditating, and I stopped to rest my eyes . . . and I guess I had a vision. The cobblestones started moving—they began coming together like jigsaw pieces to form a person . . . somebody dressed in white, like an angel. I looked closer at the angel's face—and it was your face, Bonnie. And in your arms was a tiny baby, with blue eyes and blond curly hair. . . . And I knew it was a boy." He stared back at the street. "It's gone now . . . I wonder what that's supposed to mean."

My heart was suddenly dancing. "I know what it means, dad," I announced. "I prayed just last night that if it was time for us to have a child, God would show us. And obviously, God just showed us!"

My poor father was hardly prepared for that. "Now wait a minute," he protested. "That may not have been the meaning at all—I don't want to be responsible for . . ."

"Don't worry, dad," I said cheerfully. "God just used you to confirm something to me, and I believe it."

When I went to the grocery store that afternoon, I was already planning to throw out the rest of my contraceptives. On the way back, as I approached the house, the Baptist landlady who lived on the first floor came out to greet me.

"Bonnie," she said almost right away, "I had the strangest dream about you last night. I dreamed you had the most beautiful baby. It was about two years old and had darling blond curly hair and the most beautiful blue eyes."

Brazilians tend to dote over blue eyes since they are so rare in their country.

"And Bonnie," she continued to gush, "please forgive me—but the child was *so* beautiful that I wanted to steal it from you!"

I laughed and patted her arm.

"What was it?" I asked.

Her eyes grew wide with excitement. "It was a man-child."

I thanked her for sharing her dream with me and proceeded upstairs to tell my father. He shook his head, and then got his Bible to read me the words of Joseph: "And for that the dream was doubled unto Pharaoh twice; it is because the thing is established by God, and God will shortly bring it to pass" (Genesis 41:32).

He was right. We soon knew that our firstborn was on the way, and in my heart I knew it would be a boy. His birth on September 30, 1967, was a beautiful experience without the need for painkillers, and I was conscious the entire time. I held him in my arms and spoke the name I had chosen long before: Stephan John.

We moved almost immediately after his birth to work in an orphanage in Guarulhos, a suburb of Sao Paulo, operated by the Brazilian Assemblies of God (see photo section). Day after day I kept a busy pace not only mothering my own son but caring for dozens of other children as well. Some of my time was spent teaching supplementary classes to help them catch up with their peers in the public school. My husband was involved as well in the daily demands of the orphanage.

Virtually all of the orphans had worms. A kindly Brazilian doctor donated a great deal of time and supplies to help us rid the children of up to five different kinds of worms. Unfortunately, as the time passed, I contracted a parasitic microorganism myself that produced toxoplasmosis, and the good doctor could not seem to fight it off. Then in 1969 I became pregnant again, and the battle to regain my health intensified. Toxoplasmosis is especially dangerous to the central nervous system of infants.

I began losing weight instead of gaining. I became so sick at times that I could not drink water, and I spent much of the pregnancy in a hospital bed. I fell from my normal 115 pounds to only 100 at the end of the nine months.

The only thing I knew for sure was that if God would be gracious enough to give us a little girl, her name would be Stephany, again in honor of the Jones' first daughter, the Korean war orphan.

Stephany arrived on December 5, 1969, in a hospital near the orphanage. She appeared normal for the first week, but then it became apparent that something was wrong. She did not cry, and her temperature began to drop. The days and nights passed with little improvement, and finally we went to a pediatrician. Within five minutes he announced, "You must take her to the large clinic in downtown Sao Paulo. That's her only hope."

I glanced at my husband, and in that glance the doctor

could see our hesitation. We had no car; we didn't have money for taxi fare downtown. He reached into his pocket, pulled out a roll of *cruzeiros,* and handed it to us without another word. We left for the city immediately.

The prospect of leaving Stephany there and going home alone tore at my heart. I was back early the next morning to see her, but I could get no closer than the nursery window, where I stared at her incubator and watched her turn blue as she pulled for every breath.

"Are you Stephany's mother?" a voice said behind me.

I turned to face one of the doctors who had been treating her since yesterday.

"Yes."

He looked toward the incubator for a long moment, and then made a statement without warning.

"She's dying."

I could not believe his lack of tact. Did he have to put it so bluntly? Tears began welling up inside me, and before I knew what was happening, he began to move on down the corridor.

"What do you mean?" I called after him. "She's dying now? Three days from now? A week? How long does she have?"

He stopped and shook his head as he said, "I don't know." And then he was gone.

At that point I lost all control. My husband ushered me back outside to where my parents were waiting in their van, and we returned to their home. My mother gave me a tranquilizer, which had no effect at all. A brief verse of Scripture from Psalm 121 passed through my mind as I stood gazing out the window: "I will lift up mine eyes unto the hills, from whence cometh my help. . . ." But something within me said that there was no help for Stephany; the doctor's words would prove true.

The next morning at home I began to prepare for the

inevitable. I gathered a little yellow dotted-swiss dress with five pleats down the front, a matching yellow pillow I had made, and a blanket I had made with little bears on it. Then I wrote my daughter a letter of love and affection. Though she would never be able to read it, I wanted to place it beside her anyway.

I had made the hospital staff promise to call me immediately if she died, and inside I told myself, "When she's gone, and I can finally touch her little body again, I'm going to take her to a quiet corner somewhere and just hold her as if she were alive. I'm going to take my time—thirty or forty minutes."

A few days later, the phone call came. But we discovered to our horror that Stephany had died almost twenty-four hours previous. When we got to the hospital morgue, there was no chance for the reverie I had imagined. Instead, her refrigerated body was brought out on a steel cart, wrapped only in a diaper, with ghastly incisions running down her chest and around her scalp from an autopsy. Her face was misshapen, and mucus trailed from her nose.

In the United States, I knew, burial customs would have shielded the grieving parents from such a shock. But this was Brazil, and there were no intermediaries. The hospital staff simply waited for us to take care of what was ours.

In spite of the waves of shock and anguish that were sweeping over me, I still wanted to hold her. I reached out to touch the little form on the cart, and it was like ice. The Stephany I knew was destroyed. I pulled back my hand.

My husband and father began checking to find an inexpensive cemetery plot while I prepared the body for burying. I dressed her in the little yellow dress I had brought and added a little yellow hat to cover some of the autopsy scars. Then I placed her in a cheap cardboard coffin purchased from the morgue, and wrapped the blanket with the bears around her. In one hand I placed a yellow rosebud that had bloomed in our backyard just that morning. On the other side I placed my love note.

It was time to go. They wheeled the open casket through a set of doors into a large waiting room, and suddenly a new atrocity hit my shattered nerves. There were at least fifty people in the room, and it seemed as if they all came rushing to see the body and to gasp. It was more than I could take. I pushed them aside and fell across the casket to shield my daughter from their curious eyes. At that point, a tenderhearted Brazilian began moving the cart with me still covering it toward another room, where my husband, my parents, and I had a private ceremony of Scripture and prayer, giving little Stephany back to God.

We then took the cardboard casket and drove to the cemetery. Again, swarms of children followed us to see where the foreigners would bury their dead. The casket was lowered into the ground and the dirt thrown back on top. I pushed a small cluster of pansies into the soil, and then we retreated to my parents' house.

My husband went on home ahead of me in order to clear the rooms of everything that had been Stephany's. Her buggy, her bottles—everything was gathered into her room, and the door was shut. When I arrived home later, I made a second check. Finally, night fell.

I shared in those hours a deeper affinity than ever before with Marceline Jones and all the other mothers of the world who had lost children. I could not sleep; I could only stand at the window and wonder why this tragedy had come. I remembered the statement of Job in his calamity, "Though he slay me, yet will I trust him," but at the moment I was not sure I could be so steadfast.

## THE BROKEN GOD

Presently it began to rain. I stood watching the raindrops and thinking about Stephany lying out there in the cold night. *It's raining on my baby. It's raining on my baby.*

# five THE SHOCK

THE TOXOPLASMOSIS HAD NOT YET been evicted from my body by the time we returned to the States for furlough six months later. Another struggle was going on simultaneously in my mind, as I continued grieving for Stephany. For a while, I had gone to bed each night clutching the sleeper she had worn on her last trip to the downtown hospital, just to catch the scent that lingered there. I tottered on the edge of neurosis for a while, more than my husband ever realized. Eventually, I had given Stephany's entire wardrobe to a poor Brazilian woman with a new infant. But the memories stayed.

43

In such a state, it was not at all clear that we should plunge into a year of raising funds, as most returning missionaries did, and then go back to our field of service. Both my husband and I felt dislocated, uncertain about our future. We went temporarily to be near his mother in western New York, where I took a job as a secretary to support us. Shortly after Christmas, we had accumulated enough cash to make it to the West Coast, where I had grown up. That seemed as good a place as any to try to continue to sort out our lives, our marriage, and our beliefs. We settled in an apartment in Costa Mesa, a Los Angeles suburb; I found another clerical job, and he began working part-time in a bookstore.

Eight years had now passed since I had seen Jim and Marceline, and when my mother informed me that they also had come west, I rushed to the telephone. It was a jubilant conversation, and we quickly made plans to get together the next time they came to Los Angeles for meetings. Jim explained that large groups of people from the home church in Redwood Valley came with them each time in a fleet of buses. I was welcome to ride back with them for an extended visit.

A series of affectionate letters went back and forth between us, and finally on Thanksgiving weekend, 1971, our family went to Jim's rally at the Embassy Auditorium in downtown Los Angeles. It was impressive. A large, multiracial choir sang infectious songs about brotherhood and peace and love between all God's children. The sermon emphasized the same themes. As in the past in Brazil, Jim did not lead in prayer, but I hardly noticed. I was fascinated by the crowd and the many worthy Peoples Temple projects that were described—homes for senior citizens, drug rehabilitation outreaches, tutoring programs. My only disappointment was that Marceline was not present. She, a registered nurse, had been

Second page of Jim Jones' letter to me dated September 17, 1971. Final
sentences read, "Well, I must get back to the responsibility of 508 letters today;
but I had to take a moment out again to write our beloved daughter & family.
We also hold you in the same consciousness!

"Give my love & devotion to all. We shall implement that love with
considerable action in the future.

"Eternally, Jim, Marcie & all"

tied up that weekend with her job as a state nursing home inspector.

I boarded one of the buses afterward for the overnight run up the coast, while Stephan and my husband returned home. The joyful singing continued on the bus—songs I hadn't heard before but which impressed me with their idealism. Finally I was asked what I wanted to sing.

"How about 'God is so good to me'?" I remembered Jim and Marceline singing that one in Brazil from their Indianapolis days.

No one on the bus seemed to know it. There was an awkward pause until one elderly person finally recalled the tune and the words. We eventually fell asleep as the bus rolled on through the night.

The five hundred residents of tiny Redwood Valley were still asleep when our caravan rolled in around five o'clock Monday morning. Further down the road was a bank, a post office, a Northwestern Pacific Railroad freight depot, and not much else in the darkness. Seven miles back we had passed through Ukiah, the county seat of about ten thousand. Jim and about a hundred of his Indianapolis congregation had come here in 1965. It was as close as he could settle to Eureka, California—one of the nine recommended havens from nuclear war—and still avoid the geological fault that ran in a southeasterly direction from there.

The buses were unloaded, and Jim showed me to an upstairs bedroom in their home, an attractive two-story just across from the temple. I slept until early afternoon. Marceline was still out of town in connection with her work. She returned at about six o'clock, and we rushed into each other's arms in a surge of happy tears.

At the dinner table that evening, we reveled in memories of Belo Horizonte. Their Stephan was now twelve years old, and the other boys were not far behind. I teased about how I'd baby-sat for them long ago. Jim and Marceline filled in the details of their move to Rio de Janeiro, and then before I knew it, he was into the middle of a most uncomfortable story.

He told how they had come across an orphanage in one of Rio's *favelas*—the hillside ghettos—where children were literally on the edge of starving. He was deeply concerned, and telegraphed back to Peoples Temple in Indiana for aid. But the church was in debt itself and could not help.

"Marcie and I decided we'd do anything to get money to help them," Jim continued. "And there was this wealthy woman—her husband was a Brazilian diplomat—who offered me $5,000 cash in exchange for three nonstop days of sex with her in a hotel. I didn't want to do it, but—"

I almost choked. I looked around the table, embarrassed that all the children were listening to their father speak this way . . . but they went right on eating. They had obviously heard all this before. Even Marceline didn't blanche.

"Those kids in that orphanage had to have help, and nobody else was doing anything about it," Jim continued. "So we met at the hotel and stayed in the room for three days straight. But at the end, when she went to hand me the money, I said, 'Oh, no, you don't. This isn't for me. This is for the children in the *favela*. You must go there with me and hand it to the orphanage leader yourself.' "

He went on to describe the disdain on her face as she tried to protect her white skirt while walking through the filthy orphanage. She cautiously kept the grimy hands of the children from leaving a smudge until she could deliver the money and make a quick exit.

Jim made it sound like the most magnanimous sacrifice

Jim's letter of September 24, 1971, signed "Jim and Rainbow Family."

Dear family

It was thrilling to hear from you.

I'm just leaving on a campaign. Marxie has proceeded ahead. We'll return Monday. She'll be tickled delighted & inspired knowing we've make contact once again.

Please visit us at your convenience — on the house as the saying goes anytime! Save apples for your precious folks.

Jim Pugh who owns a rest home here & loved your parents so much will be writing a note too.

Golly can't hardly wait to see you

"over"

We'll be holding a
Campaign in Los Angeles
over Thanksgiving weekend
at the Embassy auditorium
downtown L.A. Fri, Sat
& Sun. We also will
be sending one or two of
our lovely greyhound type
busses to bring some of our
L.A. members here in a few
weeks, thus if you ever
want to come that way that
too will cost you nothing.
Hurry to see us!

Deep Love in Him
Jim & Rumfar
Family

P.S.
Bless you
for the
precious
picture

(We have now
adopted a
blond headed
boy too)

of his life. My head was churning, but I thought about how far $5,000 would go in a Brazilian orphanage. Perhaps the end justified the means in an extreme case like this.

After dinner was finished, we moved into the living room to talk, and Jim and Marceline looked at each other almost immediately and then said (I don't remember which one), "Bonnie, it's so good to see you again. You know, of course, that you were our daughter in many lifetimes." I would have choked again if I hadn't been prepared by something that had happened shortly before I had left Brazil. I had been reading a book entitled *Youth, Yoga, and Reincarnation,* and when I had come to the section on reincarnation, I had shut the book almost immediately. That was anti-Christian, wasn't it?

But a few days later, I thought, "Is my faith so weak that I can't even see what this book has to say?" So I returned to the place where I had stopped, and while finishing the book, I had the distinct impression—one of those sudden bursts of intuition—that maybe I had been Jim and Marcie's daughter in an earlier life.

And now . . . here they were giving me names and a place to support my impression. "We were Pharaoh Ikhnaton and his wife, Nefertiti, back in Egypt, and you were in our family."

Ikhnaton, they said, was a heretic pharaoh of Egypt in the 1300s B.C. He dared to replace the many deities of the time with one supreme sun-god, Aton. He moved his capital from Thebes to a new, virgin site, where he built an amazing city, Amarna. He encouraged the arts, especially sculpture.

The beauty of Nefertiti, his wife, can still be seen today in the sculpture of various museums of the world. They had six daughters, one of which married a young man who succeeded Ikhnaton to the throne, the famous King

Tutankhamen. Whether I was that daughter they didn't say.

But Jim was not finished. He had also been Buddha, and Lenin, and even Jesus Christ, among others. Life was a tapestry, he explained, and each of us, as various threads, have come back to the surface again and again.

I knew my parents would have been aghast at such claims. But in my present state of mind and health, I was in no shape to resist, especially two people who meant so much to me personally. In a way, I found the discussion fascinating, bewildering; we kept talking until Marcie announced that she needed to go on to sleep. She had to get up early the next morning for work.

Jim and I stayed in the living room to talk until past midnight, and then came the third surprise of the evening. He wanted to know how my sex life was doing. I'd already hinted that my marriage was not in the best condition, but I brushed him off by saying that our physical relationship was in fine shape. His questioning persisted, and more specifically; soon he was asking how often I faked orgasms. When I said I'd never faked one in my life, he gave out with his peculiar high-pitched giggle. "I should have known," he said. After a few more questions, we retired for the night.

The next day was Tuesday, and Marceline found time to give me a tour of the various Peoples Temple projects. We saw the convalescent homes where elderly blacks and whites lived together in harmony and security. We saw the ranch for retarded children. We saw the temple-subsidized dormitories for college students in nearby Santa Rosa, which enabled young people from poor families to stay in school. The emphasis everywhere was on justice, equality, and sharing. I was impressed.

Jim presented me that day with a book that he said would basically explain his view of things: the title read,

## THE BROKEN GOD

*Introduction to Communism.* That alarmed me, but once I got into the opening chapters, I couldn't object to what was being said about the evils of class prejudice and benefits of sharing. I was very naive; I knew the Bible described how the early Christians in Jerusalem lived communally and shared whatever they had with one another without regard for race or status. Perhaps Jim was on to something good here. I couldn't quite tell how much of a place there was for God in his thinking, however. I would have to keep listening and watching.

That question was settled with a blast on Wednesday evening, when we went to the midweek service at the temple. The building had a pitched ceiling with a stained-glass window high above the platform. It was an unusual structure in that the back section was a swimming pool, but boards were laid across it so that more folding chairs could be set up when necessary to accommodate a crowd of up to 500. Behind the podium was a tall, cushioned stool from which Jim spoke, and overhead was a banner and an American flag.

A choir began with some of the same songs I had first heard in Los Angeles, backed by a lively instrument section. Jim came onto the platform in a long, black robe, which combined with his jet-black hair and his sunglasses to create a powerful image. The sunglasses also served to conceal his expressions, which tended to be quite transparent otherwise. Everyone seemed taken with his dynamic presence.

He soon began to speak. "People are hung up on God. Too many people are taken up with the golden slippers they hope to get when they fly away to heaven. In the meantime, they're absolutely useless here on earth. What Jesus wanted to do was to make a heaven right here and now. In Matthew 25 he told about all the self-righteous Christians who are going to be out in the cold because they never fed the hungry or clothed the naked or visited the prisoners."

I could agree with that. I'd been turned off by do-nothing Christianity since I was a teenager.

The sermon intensified. Before long he was shaking his fist at the American flag, calling this a nation of bigots and fascists who would someday come to wipe out groups like Peoples Temple. He then threw a Bible to the floor and said it only served to distract people from the work at hand.

And then he spit on the Bible.

"We can let nothing stop us from building a just and loving society right here on earth! We must tear down the sky God and all this talk of the sweet bye and bye!" He raised his right fist again. "If there's a God up there, ---- you, God!"

I flew out of my seat and dashed for an exit. I could not believe what I had just heard come out of Jim Jones' mouth. I didn't stop running until I got to my room, slammed the door, and collapsed on the bed. I doubled up in actual, physical pain. I broke into sobbing.

What would happen to a man who uttered such an obscenity? Suddenly I was gripped by a fear for the eternal destiny of the couple who had been such a tower of strength to me. How had Jim come to such madness?

But then . . . I thought about the practical parts of what he had said. I thought about the projects I had seen the day before. Maybe this *was* what it was all about. What if Jim was right after all? I wasn't God's attorney; in fact, I'd never settled the questions Jim had posed to me eight years before about why God, if he existed, allowed such a world of misery.

And again I was gripped by pain, because if God didn't exist . . . twenty-six years of my life had just gone down the drain. It was as if a giant arm had swept down across the chessboard of my life and sent every piece flying. It all was suddenly meaningless.

The second option was as terrible as the first. I continued to sob.

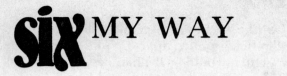

# SIX MY WAY

THERE WAS A KNOCK on the bedroom door.

"Who is it?" I sputtered. I didn't want to see anyone.

"Bonnie . . . it's Marceline."

I closed my eyes and sighed. "Please—not now, Marcie. I just want to be alone."

After a moment's hesitation, she opened the door anyway and came on in. She sat down on the edge of the bed where I still lay and began to stroke my shoulder. "I'm sorry, Bonnie. I'm really sorry you're so upset."

Her love and understanding helped to calm me after a while, and she brought me a tranquilizer of some kind. I was finally able to articulate some of what was going on inside.

"Marceline, it's like there's no secure place left for me—I feel like I'm being pulled apart by wild horses." I spelled out how awful it would be if I had been wrong all my life about God—and how awful it would be for the two of them if I had been right. "There's no way out, and I don't think I can cope with the emotional pain of it all."

She didn't try to reason further with me then; she simply mothered me until I eventually went to sleep under the power of the sedative. I had a dream that night about being forced to move from a small cottage to a much larger house, and being reluctant to do so. The thought of rearranging all my furniture and getting re-settled was overwhelming to me. When I awoke on Thursday morning, it wasn't hard to see how the dream connected with real life.

Jim continued to spend long periods of time with me that day and the next, explaining his goals and criticizing the churches for their prejudices and failure to deal with real human need. The myth of a God up in the sky, he argued, was irrelevant to the task at hand: to build a socialistic paradise where people of all races would be respected and treated with dignity and compassion.

By the time Marceline drove me to Santa Rosa on Friday to catch the plane back to southern California, my confusion and depression had plunged me to new lows. I could not refute Jim's arguments—but how could I go home and tell my husband what I'd been through and that I wasn't sure God was alive anymore? Marceline was again tender and empathetic; she wrote me a letter a few days later in which she said,

> *I want you to know that I feel the trauma that you are experiencing. As I left you at the airport, I wished I could go with you to be a buffer between you and the terrible anxiety that you must experience as you face truth and make the*

*necessary adjustment. It is painful as you go through it but gloriously rewarding after the transition is made. Do not feel that you have wasted a quarter of a century. . . . Each phase is necessary though it varies with individuals due to variations in our Karma. . . .*

She closed the letter, which was dated December 11, 1971, with this:

*Honey, the only way to face truth is one day at a time. Be true to what you believe as each incident to test it arises. When you don't know what to do—do nothing until you are sure. I have utmost confidence in your honesty and courage and—I love you very much.*

By that time I had already spilled the whole thing to my husband. He was understandably shaken. But he was also rather weak in his own faith at this point, and unable to mount a strong rebuttal. I decided I needed outside help.

I made an appointment to see a minister the next week. He was not the pastor of the church we had been attending—I wasn't sure I wanted to unload something this serious on him. Instead, I called a man who had known my family for a number of years; I felt I could trust him. Surely he would be able to defend God's case, if in fact it was defensible.

"I really need your help," I began that day as I picked him up at his home. We drove a few blocks and pulled to the curb to talk. "My faith in God has been very shaken by something that happened last week. But actually, I guess it was just the climax to what has been building over the last couple of years. As you know, I've spent part of my life in Brazil, and I've seen an awful lot of suffering and misery, and some of that suffering has come into my own life through the death of my daughter—and I'm having real doubts as to whether God even exists. . . ."

"Bonnie," he interrupted with a wave of his hand, "you're not going through anything that's terribly unusual. When I was in college, I had doubts about the existence of God myself."

I felt angry that he hadn't faced the question. It seemed entirely serious to me, but he was just brushing it aside.

Before I knew it, he had leaned closer and taken my hand in his. "Bonnie," he continued, "I'm really glad you came today, because I really love you." A look of anticipation came into his eyes. "I love you so much that I'd like to show you . . . I'd like to take you to bed with me."

I jerked my hand back, started the engine, and drove him back without uttering another word. I never saw him again. Something went *snap* on the inside of me; it was all over. I told myself, "That finishes it. I gave God one last opportunity to answer the questions I've worried about for a long time, one final chance to prove Jim Jones wrong, and what happens? God's spokesman brushes my questions aside and proceeds to proposition me! If God existed, he obviously wouldn't have let this happen."

I didn't have the heart to tell my husband about the incident, but he soon realized that I had crossed a point of no return. We went to church together only once after that, and nearly everything seemed to reinforce my opinion that it was all a sham. The congregation was entirely white except for one black man—who sat in a pew all by himself. Not another person would approach his row. In the course of the service there were three different songs about heaven. I finally leaned over to my husband and whispered, "I am never coming to church again, and you better promise not to try to hang any guilt trip on me about it, or else I'm going to stand up right now and tell these righteous people what I think about their singing all about heaven and not practicing Jesus' word about loving your brother." I wasn't bluffing; I was mad enough to do it.

"OK, OK, I promise," he whispered back. "Just don't say anything, and you don't have to come again."

I pulled on my sunglasses (my standard way of retreating from distasteful situations) and endured the rest of the service.

I cannot say that I was entirely happy with my capitulation. I remember awakening one beautifully clear, sunny morning with birds singing and flowers blooming, and recalling the words of the English poet who wrote, "God's in his heaven; all's well with the world." And suddenly I thought, "No—God's not in his heaven, and nothing is right with the world." That greatly depressed me.

But Jim Jones and Peoples Temple were attempting to make things right in the world, and they were making progress, and so they were the best of the available choices. The letters and phone calls back and forth to Redwood Valley became more frequent throughout the early months of 1972. I wrote letters to public officials at Jim's request to curry favor in high places. We attended more of his Los Angeles meetings. He proposed that we be sent at some future point to Chile to work with orphan children and also start a Peoples Temple agricultural mission—the concept that eventually became a reality in Guyana. Chile was especially attractive in those days because of its socialist regime under Salvador Allende. My husband and I, having already been missionaries in South America, seemed well suited for the task.

On May 31, 1972, I wrote the following letter to my parents.

*Dear mom and dad,*
    *Due to the issue at hand, I feel I must be completely*

*honest and frank in expressing my feelings concerning our move to Redwood Valley the third of June and my ligation with the Joneses.*

*You said in your letter I seem to think I could do exactly opposite of what you had taught me to do, and dismiss it with a word. If you taught me anything, you taught me to think for myself and to make my own decisions. I am doing that. Until this point in my life I have made decisions that you agreed with, some because I felt it was right and others I made because I wanted to please you. I am twenty-six years old now; surely if ever I am going to think for myself it is now.*

*You know that you can't drag me to heaven on your coattails. I must make my own way in life by using my own brain and making my own decisions. Otherwise, what would I do when you die? I would be a lost zombie.*

*You said you believe Jim to be a traitor to Christ and you. You couldn't have known him as well as you did and not be aware of his beliefs. He told me that when he saw you, he questioned the wisdom of letting me come up to Redwood Valley, so you knew there was some danger I would discover what he believed.*

*If, as you say, I go to a country as a missionary* [meaning Chile], *I will teach the people to get their God out of the sky and down to earth, to feed the hungry, clothe the naked, visit the sick and afflicted—to stop being hung up on heaven and its golden streets and get their religion down to earth.*

*I knew when I made my decision you would be against it; don't think that you only have suffered. You say you are sure I haven't realized all the repercussions of my decision, but you are wrong. I am not as addlebrained as you think. I pondered very deeply before coming to any conclusion.*

*This decision has cost me all: the people I love so dearly, and the country I love so deeply* [Brazil]. . . . *You said you hoped God would have mercy on us. Have you disowned me because of my decision? Is God less loving and merciful than you? Is he going to throw us into hell after we have given everything to help others? If so, I want none of his mercy; I want nothing to do with his heaven; I will burn in hell with the rest of the people who are living a more Christian life than any other Christian group I know.*

*I have sat through meeting after meeting [of Peoples Temple] and seen only good come. A house divided cannot stand. I don't believe Satan does good for any reason. My spirit is witness to me that this is good and right. I must follow after truth as I see it.*

*Be assured that nobody but my husband has read your letter. I have not been coached in writing you this letter; I'm merely writing honestly from my heart my feelings. I know they hurt you, and for that I am deeply sorry. I hope you will be able to accept my decision and know that I have made it out of the sincerity of my heart.*

*My deepest love to you both,*

*Bonnie*

The next week my husband, four-year-old Stephan, and I moved in with the Joneses in Redwood Valley until we could find a permanent place to live.

# seven GOD IN A BODY

MY IMMERSION INTO THE EVERYDAY WORLD of Peoples Temple came sooner than I had expected. Not long after we arrived, Jim announced one morning, "We're going to take the buses and all go on a two-week vacation up to Canada and then down to Mexico. We'll hold some meetings along the way, but it'll also be a great trip for the senior citizens and the children, now that school is out. Bonnie, I'd really like for you and Stephan to go along."

My husband had just gotten a job at a masonite manufacturing plant, so he was ruled out, but Stephan and I began packing our suitcases. It sounded like an enjoyable time—a chance to see some beautiful country and also to get to know people better. It took at least six buses to transport the group, which numbered more than two hundred altogether. We headed north toward meetings in the state of Washington.

Along the way I met some of the dearest elderly black people, who were now spending their sunset years in the retirement homes of Peoples Temple. Two of them became my closest friends. One called herself by the rather striking name of Love Life—it was something she had acquired in earlier years at Father Divine's mission back in Philadelphia. She was a warm, gentle woman in her eighties with failing eyesight because of cataracts; she soon became like a grandmother to me.

The other woman was even older—101—and was known as Ever Rejoicing, which described her perfectly. She cut an unforgettable profile: her nearly six-foot frame was as thin as it could be—and always topped by a champagne-blond Dutch Boy wig. She was a spunky, gorgeous lady who could entertain her listeners for hours on end.

The arrangements for food on the trip were that you could either bring your own, or else you could pay the temple a certain amount and eat what was provided. I chose the second option, and it turned out to be a bad mistake. We sometimes rode for up to twelve hours at a time, and for some reason we were not allowed off the buses even at gas stations to get coffee. Stephan kept watching the others around us pulling out their own Hershey bars and popcorn and cold chicken while his stomach growled, and he began to cry.

"Don't worry, honey," I tried to explain. "When we stop, we'll get our food."

We finally stopped in a park, and picnic tables were gathered for serving the rest of us. We waited impatiently in long lines, and the menu that first day turned out to be something like noodles and tuna out of cans—unheated. There was also some Kool-Aid to wash it down with, and some sort of cake for dessert, but altogether it was not a very appetizing meal.

As I waited, I watched one of the early ones, a young child, struggling to finish. He apparently had an upset stomach from all the traveling, and he whined to his mother that he wasn't hungry.

"No, you have to clean up your plate," she answered.

Soon Jim came over to reinforce the rule. "No one wastes good food. Every bite has to be eaten. Eat the rest, son."

The boy looked positively ill. He forced down another bite or two of cold noodles, and then his entire lunch came back up onto his plate again.

"No, no, no," Jim barked. "You're not going to get out of it that way. That's just manipulation. Eat."

And he continued to stand over the boy until his plate was clean.

I was appalled. Jim must be having a bad day, I decided, and I tried to stay out of his way from then on. When I reached the serving table, I mumbled something about not being very hungry, and so got by with a smaller-than-average helping. As I ate, I saw curly-haired little Martin Amos, who was younger than Stephan, drop some of his food into the dirt. Whether it was intentional or not I don't know, but again, Jim noticed.

"No, Martin—we can't waste food. You pick it up and eat it." And the little boy obeyed, dirt and all.

Our meeting in Washington was held in a rented auditorium, having been well advertised in advance in the newspapers. This was apparently one of Jim's frequent stops, because there were a number of local people who welcomed us into their homes for overnight. Stephan and I, along with Joyce and Dale Parks (who six years later would flee from Jonestown with Leo Ryan's party), were taken to a lovely house where we were able to take showers and wash out some clothes.

The next day we were back on the road headed for Canada, and this time we were not so fortunate. The buses pulled into an open field of high grass at about three or four in the afternoon. The field, we soon found, was infested with mosquitoes, and so we were ordered to stay on the buses for the time being.

It was hot. The air conditioning, however, was shut down. We sat and sweltered. Stephan cried. Another little boy said, "I need to get off to go to the bathroom." By this time, the bus's restroom was either broken or its tank was full and could no longer be used.

Our bus driver was an intense young man named Don Sly—the one who pulled the knife on the congressman in Jonestown. Even back in 1972, he was a zealot.

"No, you can't get off, kid. Nobody gets off."

"I can't wait—I have to go," the boy pleaded.

"No."

Soon the odor in the crowded bus became even worse than it had already been, with all the stale food and the perspiration. Supper was canceled, and we never did leave the bus that night; we slept in our chairs. By the next morning, I was sick.

My temperature began to rise, and after a while I went into delirium. I cannot remember the next two days. Others on the bus apparently took care of Stephan while I lay incoherent in my seat. When I finally came to, we had left Canada and were stopped somewhere along the way to use facilities. My first mental picture after those two days is of long lines of our people waiting outside restrooms. I was so weak I could hardly walk. Someone took my arm and helped me to join the line.

About an hour later we pulled into some tourist attraction, and everyone else piled off the buses to see it. My forehead was still burning, and I was vomiting. I remained in my seat, staring dully out the window.

A woman poked her head in the door. "What are you doing on this bus?"

"I'm sick."

"Father said *everybody* is supposed to come see this place," she announced.

I shuddered. "Well, you tell Father that I'm not going!" Not only did I not have the strength, but my moccasins had begun to unravel, and my only other footwear was in my suitcase below.

At that, she started toward me to force me out of the bus. From somewhere she came up with a pair of size 8 or 9 boots for me to wear (my feet are size 5). I was so mad I threw them back at her. But, after getting help from another woman, she still managed to pick me up by my arms and herd me outside. I had no choice but to wear the boots, and she stayed with me to hold me up as I clopped along through the entire attraction.

Jim saw me along the way and smiled. "Good to see you're up and around, Bonnie," he said as he slapped me on the back, nearly knocking me over. I was so angry that I thought, "If I had enough money, and if I could get my cases out of the luggage compartment of the bus, I would get Stephan and go home right now, no matter what anybody says." But that was impossible; I was trapped, and would have to stick it out.

My fever eventually came down, and I began to eat again as we traveled toward Mexico. The quality of the food seemed to improve somewhat as the trip continued. The miles went by quickly when we sang songs; some on the bus had brought guitars. Now that I felt better, I could again appreciate what a wonderful thing this was—to take all kinds of people black and white, from 2 to 101, on a vacation together.

All of the buses were equipped with CB radios, and one day Don Sly reported to Jim's bus, "I've seen Bonnie Burnham comb her hair twice now." He wasn't being funny; he thought it was a real infraction. Most of the others on the bus were black, and their hair didn't get blown by the wind. Don wore a crewcut. In his thinking, I was exhibiting total vanity by running a comb through my long blond hair.

I brushed it off as ridiculous, called Don an obscene name, and reminded him that Jim Jones combed and sprayed his hair more than any human being alive.

"That's different," Don replied. "He's God; he has to look perfect. People wouldn't understand if he had hair in his eyes."

The buses rolled on across the border into Mexico, past Tijuana and Ensenada, and stopped that night at a beach along the Pacific. It took some arguing with the local Mexican authorities before we got permission to camp there. We finally began unrolling our sleeping bags and setting up a few tents for the very oldest folk such as Ever Rejoicing. While other senior citizens preferred to sleep on the buses, she never missed a chance to prove her spunk by using her sleeping bag.

Then someone came around with the news that Stephan would spend the night with someone else.

"Absolutely not," I said. "Why should he have to do that?"

"He needs to learn to relate to other people. He's too dependent on you."

"Listen—he doesn't even speak English very well. None of you speak Portuguese, which is what he learned growing up in Brazil." We had spoken Portuguese even at home while at the Sao Paulo orphanage, and it had become Stephan's first language.

Jim came along to assure me. "Bonnie," he said, "he's been spoiled, you know. All he knows is you. You must let him relate to others; this is our socialist way, and you're going to have to conform."

And so he was taken off to sleep next to a kind-looking black woman, screaming as he went, *"Mamae, mamae, mamae!"* ("Mommy!" in Portuguese).

I cried myself to sleep that night alone on the cold sand, and early the next morning, I went hunting for him. We hugged each other and sat down to eat breakfast together. After the meal was finished, he stood up with a smile and said, "Well, I'm going back to my black mother now"! He didn't seem nearly as upset as I was. The woman had been very loving and tender with him, and I thought to myself, "Well . . . maybe Jim's right after all. Maybe he really does need to find out that there are other people in the world who can love him."

That was the day I first discovered that Jim, too, believed in getting his love from several sources. The sun grew hot, and the beach had no trees for shade, and I eventually went to find shelter back on the buses. I happened to approach Jim's bus first.

There was a guard at the door. "I'm sorry," he announced, "no one's allowed on the buses."

"Why not?"

He didn't answer me, but as I looked past him and through the open door, I saw Jim and one of the young women from the group. Suddenly I knew why, and my heart was sick. This explained the coldness I had sensed in Jin and Marceline's relationship. I remembered back to Thanksgiving, when I had first seen them again, and how they hadn't hugged or kissed even though they had been apart for an entire weekend. They had just passed one another in the hall without any show of affection.

What I didn't know that day on the Baja beach was that Marceline had already been blackmailed into silence. I learned years later that when Jim first began his extramarital liaisons back around 1968, Marcie had decided to divorce him. Jim had stopped her dead in her tracks with one sentence:

"If you ever try to leave me, you'll never see your children alive again." And she knew he meant it.

Marceline Jones lived under the torment of that sentence all the way to Jonestown.

So we stayed out, broiling in the Mexican sun all day. We were incredibly sunburned; my nose and face peeled for days afterward. There was great discomfort on all sides—but Father had had his pleasure, and that was what counted.

And who was to argue? Mere mortals were subject to criticism, but when you were God incarnate, you did what you liked. Jim Jones was, in the phrase of one corpulent woman in her seventies beside whom I sat on the way home, "God in a body." She was lovable but none too bright, and she was given to reciting those four words at the most unexpected times.

We were rolling northward in the middle of the night toward Redwood Valley, with all the interior lights out and almost everyone sleeping. I gently crawled over her legs to get to the aisle and use the restroom, then returned and slipped back into my seat. Apparently I disturbed her slumber just enough for her mind to respond; I was getting my earplugs ready to insert so I could get some sleep myself when, without warning, the woman screamed at the top of her lungs:

"God in a body!"

Loud noises have always startled me, and I screamed just as loudly as she had. The entire bus woke up, Don Sly

69

turned on the lights, and there was general bedlam for a few minutes. I was chewed out by everyone for interrupting their sleep, and my face was crimson.

Finally everyone calmed down, quit swearing, and began to nestle down again as the lights were turned off. My heartbeat edged back toward its normal rhythm as I prepared my earplugs once again in the darkness. I took a deep breath and closed my eyes.

"God in a body!"

And again I shrieked in terror, and the lights came on, and the busload of people stormed and groused and swore, except for Grace Stoen, who was convulsing in laughter. Fortunately, that was the end of the outbursts; if it had happened again that night, we both would probably have been put off the bus on the spot.

The trip, of course, made good publicity for the crowds in future meetings and for the donors on the mailing list. They were told that when Jim Jones went on vacation, he didn't take just his immediate family—he took everyone. How many little black children from the ghetto got a free, all-expenses-paid trip to Mexico? Such were the benefits of the love and compassion of Peoples Temple.

# eight THE RELIGIOUS MASQUERADE

BACK IN REDWOOD VALLEY, my life soon fell into a pattern of vigorous service to the cause. Some of the members of the congregation found us an apartment in nearby Ukiah, and I soon went to work for Gene Chaikin one of two Peoples Temple lawyers.

I was not paid for my work; we lived on what my husband earned at the factory, and even 25 percent of that was contributed to the temple. Stephan was enrolled in kindergarten that fall, and I found time to visit Love Life and Ever Rejoicing. I would take carloads of black senior citizens to Lake Mendocino for picnics, or to my place for ice cream. Whenever we trooped into a cafe for sandwiches and coffee, we were quite a sight—one young white woman with five to eight ancient black ladies, including Ever Rejoicing in her wig.

Gene Chaikin had left a fairly successful law practice to join Peoples Temple, much to the consternation of his parents. He and his wife, Phyllis, asked us at one point to spend a weekend with them visiting his parents and vouching for the temple's legitimacy. We tried to assuage their fears by telling them that we had been missionaries in Brazil and now felt completely positive about this group. Where else, we asked them, could you find the outcasts of society being helped in such a practical, loving way? Where else were destitute people being fed and clothed and housed in security without condescension?

After a week of work, the normal thing on Friday night was to go to the temple for a long meeting. When it finally ended, we would load onto the buses for the three-hour ride down to San Francisco, where another meeting would begin at 11:00 A.M. The buses were always jammed, and we soon learned to stretch out however we could—in the aisles, under the seats, even in the overhead luggage racks or underneath in the baggage compartments. At least one could get into a comfortable position there.

Upon arrival, we would wash up and change clothes in the restrooms of the temple, a large building on Geary Street in the Fillmore district across from the Japanese Trade Center. The meetings would go on until eleven that night, stopping only for mealtime breaks, when tasty food prepared by the ladies of Peoples Temple was available for purchase. We were forbidden to go out to restaurants; our business was needed to help subsidize the trip. Stands were also set up in the foyer to sell pictures of Jim that would protect the buyer from harm on the highway and wherever else he might be.

Late that night, we would reboard the buses for the

nine-hour run to Los Angeles, where the same thing would be repeated. However, the meetings would usually end around six in the evening, so we could make it back to Redwood Valley in time for work and school on Monday morning. This was not an occasional jaunt; it was the standard weekend schedule, except for special times when the big-city congregations were invited to Redwood Valley for the weekend. Then we stayed home and hosted large numbers of them in our homes.

But I was a missionary's daughter; I was used to hardship. The point of life was not to have fun; the point was to *do something* for the needy of the world. And Peoples Temple was doing something.

Local teachers complained, of course, that the Peoples Temple children seemed dull and fatigued in school, especially on Mondays. Stephan didn't seem to be as affected as many of the older ones, whose schoolwork was more substantive. My husband usually had to work Saturdays and thus couldn't go along. But Jim soon found important things for me to do in the services, and thus I rarely missed a weekend on the road.

I was in charge of lining up the testimonials for each service. I made lists of those who could be trusted (mostly core members from Redwood Valley) to stand up and tell how Peoples Temple had put their lives back together after society had pushed them down, kicked them around, and cast them out. They would describe in three to five minutes each how the influence of Jim Jones had enabled them to beat their drug habit, be proud of their blackness, or find meaning and purpose in life.

I took my turn at the microphones as well, telling the audience, "Until black people are accepted without racism and bigotry in the United States, I will remain ashamed of Norwegian heritage and blond hair. Eleven o'clock on Sunday morning is still the most segregated

73

hour of the week in America. Only in Peoples Temple do you find a real, living Christlike example of what Jesus talked about, and I'm proud to be a part of it."

The atmosphere of the meetings was similar to the faith healing campaigns of the 1940s and '50s in which Jim had been nurtured. Only the words themselves betrayed the fact that this was in no way a Christian movement. It was convenient to keep the religious masquerade for at least three reasons. First of all, it kept the FBI at a distance. Secondly, it provided tax exemption. Thirdly, it brought general good will from important government officials and the public who saw our many good works. Jim was very astute; he flaunted the name of the Disciples of Christ, the denomination that had ordained him back in Indianapolis, and which amazingly continued to give credentials to his church long after he had stopped believing in God.

The meetings began with music from soloists as well as a choir of 150 young people, the girls in long blue dresses and the boys in dark trousers and shirts with ties. When they began to belt out a favorite such as "Brotherhood is our religion, for democracy we stand . . . ," they would sway to the beat and bring the crowd alive. Some very creative people in the group wrote excellent songs about peace and love and equality, and their tunes were mingled with others that had been brought from Father Divine's mission.

The children formed another choir. It was a truly moving sight to see them singing all together, black and white, brown and mulatto, Korean and Indian, their faces shining. Sometimes Marceline would sing a touching solo called "Black Baby" about her Afro-American son, Jimmy, and how she hoped to shield him from the cruelties of a racist society.

Then, after the music and the testimonials, Jim would

appear from backstage in his robe and sunglasses. He would begin with "revelations" about various people in the audience, to show his supernatural powers. It was sometimes hard to know what was truly remarkable and what was phony. Jim Jones definitely had a metaphysical talent. My father told me once about visiting the Joneses back in Brazil, when they lived on the tenth floor of a hotel along the Copacabana in Rio de Janeiro. Jim stood looking out the window at the street below, where three ladies sat waiting for a bus.

"Watch what I can do," he told my parents. "I'll make the woman in the middle stand up and walk around."

My parents watched. In a couple of seconds, the middle woman stood up and walked over to the curb.

"Now I'll make her sit down," Jim said.

She immediately sat down.

"Now I'll make her get up again."

The woman rose and walked around a little more.

"Now I'll make her sit down."

She sat.

Jim went through the routine a third time successfully, leaving my parents convinced that he held an unusual power of some kind.

On another day Jim wanted to prove his superiority by jumping from their hotel apartment and landing unhurt. Marceline talked him out of that one.

So in the meetings, Jim would proceed to call individuals out of the crowd and tell them personal details about themselves—where they worked, what medications they were taking, who their parents were and where they lived. The only trouble was, some of those on the inside knew his sources of information. Every time they stayed in the homes of temple members, they were diligent to wait until their hosts went to bed and then sneak around the house reading mail, checking prescription labels in medicine chests, and so forth. They also checked people's garbage. Then they wrote reports to be turned in to Jim.

(Even our apartment in Ukiah was ransacked at one point by Linda Amos, who somehow had gotten a key. Perhaps a duplicate had been made at the very beginning when the apartment had been rented for us. A three-page report went to Jim—mostly trivia from letters lying around, which he never did use in a "revelation." In later years, a defector from Peoples Temple gave me a carbon copy of that report.)

From the "revelations," Jim would move into the offering. Unless political dignitaries were present, this usually turned into a lengthy affair of up to an hour or even an hour and a half; most of us hated it and tried to find excuses to step out. He would begin with the large amounts first—donations of $500—and then, having gotten all he could at that level, move down to $400, and so forth. Donors raised their hands and turned over their gifts to ushers as he went along.

One particular time Jim said, "I want everybody in this church to write out a check for $100. We're not leaving here until you do. You owe God this much. You people have been stingy; you've been holding back. I don't care if you have to borrow the money—write the check now." That was exactly what happened. I wrote the check and went to the bank on Monday morning to get a loan to cover it.

Then came Jim's speaking, which tended to ramble. There was no outline or order; he flowed with the whims of the moment. He often railed about the Jews and Hitler, warning that the United States of America was becoming a similar fascist country about to commit genocide against the Afro-American race. All blacks were soon to be killed or else put into concentration camps. So the only logical thing to do was to give your money and other assets to Peoples Temple now in order to establish a safe utopia in another place, before the fascists came and confiscated it all anyway.

Jim sometimes called me out of the crowd to say, "Here's a young woman whose father was a missionary, who was raised to believe in God, and when she began to doubt that, and went to a minister to get help, all she got was a proposition to go to bed with him. Isn't that true, Bonnie?"

And I would nod my head.

His rhetoric was greatly tamed, of course, whenever public dignitaries came to visit. Then the emphasis became more positive and innocuous. Some of the blacks would be called to do ethnic dances while the crowd cheered. Jim would praise the politician for his noble deeds in the interests of the poor and oppressed, and the rafters would shake with a standing ovation.

But one day, George Moscone, the future mayor of San Francisco who had become Jim's friend, showed up unannounced. We usually had warning that public officials were coming and would shape the meeting accordingly. This time the service was already in progress when he walked into the foyer.

Upstairs, Jim was berating the crowd. "All you sanctimonious hypocrites, all you religious idiots who have gone your whole life believing in the Bible and Jesus Christ and God—I'm sick of your hypocrisy! I want you to come down off your pedestals and learn about the gut level of life! Get down where it's really at. Come on now—everybody say 'S--t!' "

A few people timidly whispered it.

"No, no, come on, *everybody!* You've got to break down your barriers. It's good for you—now yell it out!"

We yelled.

"Again!"

# THE BROKEN GOD

We yelled it again. Soon he had us chanting the one word over and over again—fourteen hundred people, old ladies, kids, rich people, poor people. After about five minutes of chanting, the place was fairly reverberating when a messenger came rushing across the stage to whisper something in Jim's ear.

Immediately he cut us off. "We have a surprise visit today, ladies and gentlemen, from someone whom we all love very much, George Moscone. . . ." and we broke into applause as he was ushered to his place wondering why he had been detained in a downstairs office so long. The children were brought to the front to charm us all with "Brotherhood is our religion. . . ."

Barring such fiascos (even Jim howled with the rest of us about it afterward), he would finish his oratory and then move into the crowd to heal. My assignment was to precede him up the aisle, walking backward so I could face him, carrying a covered tumbler of water—I always had to see where the water had come from in order to verify that it hadn't been poisoned—a comb for his hair, and a damp cloth to wipe the perspiration from his face. Surrounded by bodyguards, he moved with his microphone on the end of a long cord to touch people and dispel their sicknesses. Marceline, being a nurse, had stocked his medical vocabulary with numerous multisyllabic terms of various ailments, which he employed with a flourish. People shouted and swayed under his touch, and often claimed to be rid of their diseases. I must admit that I was not aware of the animal parts he used wrapped in a towel to pretend to be "cancers" that had been passed. But I do remember the day a crusty old woman named Janie Brown was called out of a meeting by two of the Peoples Temple nurses. She was told that her welfare agent wanted to see her downstairs. She objected, but they talked her into leaving anyway.

Once she got downstairs, the nurses said, "Father's worried about your arm."

"Nothing's wrong with my arm."

"Oh, yes—we better take you over to the hospital," they replied, and before Janie Brown knew what was happening, the nurses had talked the hospital staff into casting her arm without taking any X rays. Then she was returned to the temple, where the meeting was still in progress.

"What's that, Janie Brown?" Jim cried when he saw her walk in. "Ain't nobody gonna be in *here* with a broken arm. Marceline, you go get some surgical scissors. We're takin' that cast off right now."

She was brought to the front, where Jim said some hocus pocus over her, and Marceline proceeded to cut off her new cast. "Now, Janie, let's see you throw this across the platform," Jim said, handing her a small object. She pitched it into the crowd. The audience surged to its feet screaming. Jim Jones had performed another miracle.

But the capstone was yet to come. Near the end of many meetings, Jim would mesmerize the crowd by producing the stigmata of Christ. He would pace through the crowd with his hands upraised, blood streaming from his palms. Whether it was a sleight-of-hand trick caused by the crushing of capsules with his fingers I do not know. All I can say is that at the time, it totally convinced me that if ever there was a God, he was our God for the twentieth century. I would break into tears. He stood as a tragic martyr, shedding his blood before our very eyes. He was our one valiant hope, and we would die for his cause.

# nine FATHER KNOWS BEST?

MY PRIVILEGED POSITION as the much-heralded "daughter" of Jim and Marceline was both a blessing and a liability at Redwood Valley. It gave me ready access to "Father," but it also tended to make me a bit unpopular at times among the congregation's rank and file.

Thus it wasn't surprising that I was occasionally accused of misdeeds at the regular "catharsis" meetings. These were times when we gathered in the temple to confront each other with infractions of the rules. The meetings would start around seven or seven-thirty in the evening and usually lasted quite late.

"Bonnie's trying to be too glamorous," someone once complained. "She keeps trying to look like Zsa Zsa Gabor."

I shot back some sarcastic rejoinder, and soon the discussion moved along to other charges. On another occasion a rather large girl accused me of eating two sausages during an overnight stay at a temple member's house in Los Angeles. Sausage was on the forbidden list. But I cut that down by pointing out that the accuser had also been present and had eaten six.

Jim was not so harsh in these days as he later became, when catharsis sessions included public paddlings and rounds of boxing. He did get upset one night, however, when a group of rather straight-laced Pentecostal women were visiting, and the charges began to get personal. Someone remarked that Jim's son Jimmy had gotten a new pair of tennis shoes, in spite of the frequent claim that the Joneses always got along with hand-me-downs and thrift-store bargains. "Maybe Jim Jones never gets anything new, but his kids sure do," the man added.

Jim was about to reply when a woman piped up.

"Well, what really - - - - - - me off is—"

"Child! Child!" Jim roared as the visitors gasped. "How many times have I told you to watch your language!" And then he blurted the Portuguese aphorism he had learned in Brazil: *"Lava roupa suja em casa"* ("Wash the dirty clothes at home"). Whenever Jim didn't want a subject discussed, he would use that phrase, and we all knew to clam up.

In the absence of guests, however, there were no holds barred at Redwood Valley. The Friday night meetings there were noticeably more frank and crude than anything that ever occurred in San Francisco or Los Angeles. Jim would find places in his rambling "sermons" to point out the women in the congregation with whom he had slept and how inept they were. He would bemoan the largeness of his phallus and how every woman in the church was lusting to have her turn. Most digusting were his gestures to demonstrate his lovemaking techniques.

With hindsight, it is hard even for me to justify why I stayed around. The degeneracy of Peoples Temple stood in sharp contrast to the good it was doing for the poor, the elderly, the sick, and the misunderstood. All I can say is that at this point in my life, Jim Jones was the only game in town. I had shut off Christianity once and for all. The society at large was thought to be hostile, racist, and dangerous. So I stayed, trying to suppress the degrading aspects and think mostly about what was admirable.

He told the Temple Planning Committee that I was hot after his body like all the rest, but the truth is, he never did try anything illicit with me. In light of my fierce loyalty to Marceline, I think I would have killed him if he had. One night after a meeting, as he was walking me to my car, he accused my father of having molested me as a child. I simply swung around and swore at him. He never tried to tell me that again.

He did, however, ask for my services in trying to compromise a newspaper columnist, the Reverend Lester Kinsolving, whose caustic articles about Peoples Temple appeared in the *San Francisco Examiner* in September, 1972. "His sturdy sentries," Kinsolving wrote, "lend the temporal assurance that the Temple of The Prophet is the best-armed house of God in the land." In another article he dubbed Jim the "Ukiah Messiah" and chided the Disciples of Christ denomination for doing nothing to investigate "this amateurish, soap opera salvation" cult.

We had picketed the San Francisco newspaper for eighteen hours after that, and soon afterward, back in Redwood Valley, Jim and I were alone talking one day.

"Do you think you could seduce Kinsolving and get him off our back?" he asked.

I had been faithful to my husband up to this point, in spite of all the bed-hopping that was going on throughout the congregation. The sheep were naturally following the example set by their shepherd. But this was different.

"Sure, Jim—if you think it'll do any good, I'll be glad to."

Nothing was ever arranged, however, and the Kinsolving pressure eventually blew over.

Deep down underneath, I am not sure Jim really wanted to use his "darling daughter" in that way after all. He was a ruthless manipulator of people, but sometimes he seemed to draw the line. One night in the service he began a harangue about the need to share sex with everyone.

"What about all these old people?" he thundered. "I know what's going on—you're all jumping into bed with the good-looking ones. Who's going to care for these wrinkled old ladies and old men? Some of them haven't had a good toss between the sheets in years.

"You talk about your love for socialism. Are you willing to share with somebody who doesn't look so good?"

He was making sense, I thought. Why should we be selfish and just chase after the attractive ones? I sat there looking around and finally picked out the most shriveled, old, toothless, dimwitted black man in the place. He was eighty-seven years old and a bit loud-mouthed, but maybe he could improve with some loving.

I approached Jim in the parking lot after the service. "I know what you said is right," I began. "It's selfish for us just to be thinking about the good-looking folks. So if you'll arrange it, I'll be glad to go to bed with Mr. _____ and try to make him feel good." I actually meant it.

A smile crept across Jim's face, and he never did answer me directly. He just gave me a squeeze and said, "That's sweet." He never made any arrangements.

On a later occasion he deliberately tried to shield me from a messy situation in front of the congregation. A black teenager named Douglas had been brought to Redwood Valley after considerable trouble with the law. Jim called him to the platform and then asked for a volunteer to house him.

"Douglas has been in a lot of trouble," he explained. "He's been caught stealing. He's also been caught having sex with other boys. A lot of other people have given up on him. But we're going to help him. Who's willing to take Douglas into your home?"

I stood up. After all, this was what Peoples Temple was all about—reaching out in kindness and concern to those who needed it. Maybe we could help reverse the course of his life.

Jim went right on talking. I was standing right in the front row of the temple, but he seemed not to see me at all. He kept asking for a volunteer to shelter Douglas. *Why is he ignoring me?* I wondered. *Doesn't he think I'd be a good mother?*

After a few minutes, the crowd began talking back to Jim.

"What's wrong with Bonnie? She's been standing there for five minutes. Why don't you want her to do it?"

So Douglas came to live with us, and I soon realized why Jim had been trying to spare me. Douglas was indeed homosexual. He enjoyed watching me put on my makeup in the mornings and kept asking to try some himself. Once while putting away his laundry in his dresser, I came upon a large stack of the most incredible pornography. We finally realized we weren't making much of a dent in his life, but he certainly made a dent in

Jim Jones as he looked shortly before coming to Brazil in early 1962.

My farewell portrait for the Joneses when I left for college.

I moved in to help care for the four young children: (clockwise from lower right) Jimmy, Lou, Suzanne, and Stephan. Also pictured (upper right) is Agnes, an older adopted daughter.

CASA DA CRIANCA
LIRIO DOS VALES
FACA TAMBEM O SEU DONATIVO
AJUDE-NOS A AMPARAR UMA CRIANCA

Back in Brazil as a missionary, I spent most of my term (1966-70) working at this orphanage near Sao Paulo.

My son, Stephan, and I at Redwood Valley, California, after I had joined Peoples Temple.

Inside the Redwood Valley Peoples Temple, the banner read, "Father"—meaning Jim Jones—"we thank thee."

The Jones boys in September, 1972: (left to right) Stephan, Tim, Lou, Jimmy.

My role model: Marceline Jones.

Jim and my Stephan in
1972 at Redwood
Valley. In the
background (below),
the Peoples Temple
buses, which carried us
to meetings in San
Francisco and Los
Angeles each weekend.

The Jones family in 1975. Standing, left to right: Lou,
Stephan, Mike Cartmill (a son-in-law), Tim, Suzanne,
Jimmy. Seated: Marceline and Jim Jones. Kneeling:
Agnes and her four children.

Once we arrived in Georgetown, Guyana, we headquartered at the Pegasus Hotel.

Concerned relatives in the group included (left to right) Sherwin Harris, Clare Bouquette, and Howard Oliver; also shown is Charles A. Krause of the *Washington Post.*

Congressman Leo Ryan speaks to the group, while Sherwin Harris studies the list of some 300 faked signatures on the statement disinviting us to Jonestown.

Moments before leaving for Jonestown on Friday afternoon, Anthony Katsaris (right) waits in the hotel lobby. Tim Stoen (left) and Sherwin Harris (center) had to stay behind due to the size of the plane.

Over the threshold in the arms of my wonderful husband, Hank, on June 17, 1978.

Working on the book with Dean Merrill a few days after my return from Guyana.

our reputation in the neighborhood during the three months before he was moved to another situation. The other apartment dwellers suddenly stopped speaking to us or even looking our direction when we met on the walk.

But we were almost too busy to notice. My husband had begun to work the midnight shift, and I was as consumed as always with my secretarial work, with meetings, and the weekend trips. Our marital communication was basically a matter of notes left on the dresser.

More than once Jim concluded our meetings—at around three in the morning—by passing out slips of paper and directing everyone present to write out our ultimate commitment: "I, Bonnie Burnham, am willing to kill, destroy, and commit any other act necessary to overthrow the government of the United States of America and establish communistic rule under Jim Jones," or some such promise. Our signed papers were then filed away, and many a would-be defector thought twice about what Jim might do with those statements if a break were ever to be made. Many people assumed that they could be put in prison for life on the basis of such a document.

It was in the same meetings that we talked about the potential need for a mass suicide. We assured one another that we would rather die than be taken into fascist concentration camps. We expected to move to a safe haven in another country before America collapsed, but if we didn't, we all agreed that, yes, we'd commit suicide.

The actual practice rituals had not yet begun back in 1972 and 1973, but the thought was already born.

Some of the most moving moments came at the end of the meetings in Redwood Valley when we would link arms around each other and sway to the benediction of the national anthem of the Soviet Union: "United forever in friendship and labor . . . long live our socialist motherland, built by the peoples' mighty hand. . . ." It was a haunting melody that expressed our dreams, our dedication, and our loyalty.

At the same time, as time wore on, I found myself struggling with deeper and deeper bouts of depression. I could no longer believe in my government; I could no longer believe in the God of my childhood. My marriage was crumbling, and at times I wasn't even sure of my sexuality. One meeting after a particularly lewd string of comments, Jim said, "Everybody here except me is either a homosexual or a lesbian. Does anyone disagree with that? If you do, stand up—I'm going to wipe the floor with you."

No one moved—except me. I just could not sit still for that. I stood up and said, "That's a bunch of bull."

He whipped off his sunglasses as his face turned beet red. "Anarchist! Anarchist!" he screamed. "My own daughter's an anarchist!" A messy scene followed, and he promised to settle things with me after the meeting.

"Look, Bonnie," Marcie began once we were seated in their living room a few hours later, "you can't ever disagree with Jim in public. That just causes seeds of doubt in other people's minds. If you ever have doubts, come to Jim or me in private, but don't say it publicly."

"I understand the problem," I replied, "but if Jim doesn't want disagreement, he'd better stop asking for it. I wouldn't have said a word if he hadn't said, 'Does anyone disagree with that?' I would just have kept still. But if he asks for feedback, he's going to get it."

"No, Bonnie," she insisted, "you don't understand. What you did was a dangerous thing, and don't ever do it again."

Jim occasionally helped us all forget such scenes by

coming to the meeting in an exceptionally jolly mood. One night he walked in and surprised us all by saying, "Tonight, we're just going to have fun. Fold up the chairs—the band's going to play, and we're all going to dance." Peoples Temple suddenly turned into a club; we danced, and danced, and danced, and danced. Some didn't know how, and they just jogged to the music, while others of us were all over the floor. Jim either did his special Indian dance that always delighted the crowd, or else he sat like a doting father with a grin on his face watching the revelry. We danced far past midnight, until the perspiration was dripping off us and we looked like we'd just been dunked in the swimming pool.

But on other nights Jim's mood would be the opposite, and we would try to lift his depression by singing his favorite song, a Beatles tune called "Imagine There's No Heaven." It expressed perfectly his philosophy of refusing to look to the next world and concentrating instead on improving this one.

I had enough trouble, however, fending off my own despair. Each morning as I drove to work at Gene Chaikin's office, I came to a blind railroad crossing. It had no flashing lights, so a stop sign had been erected to force drivers to check carefully for trains.

A train came by every morning at about the time I passed that way, and as I became progressively more upset and confused, I began running the stop sign each morning, hoping that I would be hit by the train and be killed. Day after day I went zipping straight through, but the timing was always off.

One night in the middle of a service in Los Angeles, Jim suddenly stopped for a "revelation." He took off his glasses and glared down at where I sat.

"And *you*," he said as he pointed his finger, "every morning on your way to work, you're not stopping at the railroad stop sign. You're driving right on through, hoping a train will run over you. I want you to start stopping at that sign and quit this suicidal death wish."

I slunk down in my seat. He hadn't called me by name, so perhaps some of the audience would be unsure about who he had pointed to. I had no idea how he knew; perhaps his metaphysical powers were functioning once again. All I knew was that I felt tremendously embarrassed and ashamed. I began stopping from then on.

My confusion poured itself out about this time in a poem I wrote called "The Real Me." The first three stanzas went as follows:

> Who is the real me?
> Gentle, generous, kind and loving,
> Mother, sister, friend to those in need,
> Angry, rebellious, tearing lion, fishwife
> Who, did he exist, would spit in God's face
> I don't know.
>
> Who is the real me?
> Tender, caring, serving, giving,
> Innocent and honest as a child,
> Worldly-wise, suspicious of all,
> Old and haggard, no reason to live
> I don't know.
>
> Who is the real me?
> Loving nature, every breath I breathe,
> Every sound I hear, every living thing,
> Hating my very existence, whatever
> Circumstance brought me about,
> Longing for complete and eternal oblivion
> I don't know.

*Eternal oblivion.* I wanted nothing so badly as I wanted simply not to be anymore. I identified with Marceline when she sometimes said that if she could choose to be any animal, it would be a turtle. She longed to escape the constant press of people, the long hours, the demands of being the wife of Jim Jones. I had caught a taste of that when, a few months before, I had cut my hair short in a sudden fitful attack on pretense and vanity—and once it began to grow out a little, I found myself looking very much like Marceline, whose hair was usually short. For a while the elderly people would get the two of us confused and would besiege me with their aches and pains and complaints and hurt feelings. "Please tell Father that . . ."

Now my hair had grown out again, but I still wanted to pull under my shell and turn off living. I was not interested in returning to my former life as a Christian, but I didn't know how much longer I could stand this, either. Oblivion would be so welcome.

# ten THE END OF THE SHAM

IT WAS ONLY A MATTER OF TIME now, not only for my involvement with Peoples Temple, but for my marriage as well.

My husband and I had read a popular book called *Open Marriage*, which suggested that sexual fidelity was expendable in marriage. "Man is not monogamous by nature," it said. We decided to give each other permission to have affairs without letting that disturb our other reasons for staying together—economics, companionship, Stephan, and so forth. If he found somebody he was interested in, he was free to check her out, and the same went for me.

*The End of the Sham*

So it is not surprising that when a close aide of Jim's began stopping by in the late evenings while my husband worked, I welcomed the friendliness. He had been sensitive to my tiredness in San Francisco one night, asking how I felt, and we continued to enjoy one another's company over coffee in my apartment in Ukiah.

What I didn't know was that he had been sent by Jim. "Look—Bonnie's acting rather suspicious," he'd been told. "We can't afford to lose her; she's too valuable. Her relationship with her husband is falling apart, so why don't you try to satisfy her physically, and also see what you can find out?"

His visits were a bright spot in my otherwise crumbling world, and after about three months we fell into bed together four or five times. Unfortunately for Jim, the attraction was mutual, and the reports coming back were not as informative as he had hoped. Instead of getting hard data about my plans and thinking, Jim was getting only smiles and trivia.

Finally one night at three in the morning, the telephone awakened me out of a dead sleep. One of Jim's mistresses, a member of the Temple Planning Committee, was in a great state of feigned agitation. "Bonnie! We just got this terrible phone call—they've dropped off this terrible tape recording of you and _____ on your couch together. Oh, tell me it isn't true!"

I was hardly awake. "What are you talking about?"

"Someone is coming to take care of Stephan. You get dressed and get to the temple right away!"

By the time I pulled on some jeans and a shirt, temple members were at my door to drive me from Ukiah to Redwood Valley to face the committee. There sat Jim and fifteen or so members with hands folded, staring at the harlot as she walked in. Many of them, of course, were making it with all kinds of partners, too, but you never would have known it to look at them.

Jim opened the proceedings. "We have received a terrible tape recording, Bonnie—for God's sake, don't ever let Marcie know."

"Let me hear the tape."

"Oh, Bonnie," someone said, "don't do that to yourself. It would be much too humiliating."

"No, no," I said, "I can take it. Go ahead—play the tape."

They wouldn't do it. I never did learn whether there actually was a tape or not.

"Bonnie, this is really serious," Jim intoned.

I was at the point of not caring anymore. I threw them all off stride by saying, "Well, it's true." I gave my hair a toss and stared back at them.

"What are you going to do now? Have you made plans for a divorce?"

"No, not really. All I know is I like him and I enjoy being with him."

"Don't you know that this man is a known homosexual?"

I refused to be repentant. "No, I didn't know that, and I don't especially care."

Jim threw up his hands in frustration. I had refused to beg for mercy. He could see his control over me melting away. The only tactic left was intimidation.

"Well, *they*" (which at Peoples Temple usually meant the FBI or some other fascist enemy) "sent us this tape and said that if you're not out of Peoples Temple in a week, you should fear for your life."

It was a poor bluff, but I fell for it. His reverse psychology worked. I looked Jim right in the eye and said, "Fine. That settles it. I'll stay"—which was what he had wanted all along. With that, the meeting broke up.

But once I got a chance to reflect on what had transpired, I knew more strongly than ever that a change had to come. I managed to hang on for another couple of months. The end came in the wee hours of the morning after a meeting. The announcement had been made, "If any of you have any questions you'd like to ask Father, get in line, and he'll answer you one by one."

I stood in line for a long time, holding my heavy six year old as he slept on my shoulder, and forming my questions in my mind:

1. Were we going to be sent to Chile or not? We'd had nothing but postponements and delays on the project the whole time.

2. Why the double standard on sex? Why the prohibitions on sexual relations even between husbands and wives when all kinds of adultery were going on simultaneously?

3. Why had he set me up sexually with his aide? If he wanted to know what I was thinking, why didn't he ask me directly?

The line moved slowly. Finally around three-thirty, I reached the front, only to be confronted by a woman who was screening all the questioners.

"What do you want to ask?"

"I have questions for Jim," I said, "questions about promises he has made that only he can answer. Obviously, I've stood in line this long to ask Jim, not you."

She turned to look at him for what to do next.

He simply folded his arms in his robe. And then he said, "There are exceptions for no one."

So that was the way he would treat his "precious daughter." I was tired and I was furious all at once. I spun around and ran straight to my car. He called my name as I ran, but I didn't stop. I had just left Peoples Temple for the last time, I told myself.

I went home, put Stephan to bed, and tried to wash Jim

Jones completely out of my memory. I knew that defecting from the temple was a risky choice, but I had taken all I could stand.

The next morning, Jim was on the phone. "What happened, Bonnie?"

"I left—that's what happened."

"What were the questions you wanted to ask?"

"It doesn't matter, Jim. I'm never coming back to Peoples Temple."

His voice grew dark. "You're going to die, and it will look like an accident."

I refused to be intimidated. "So what?" I said, and hung up.

The next day, Marceline came to see me. We sat together in my apartment, talking. I still loved this woman, and I loved the ideals that she stood for, but we had come to a fork in the road.

"Jim's worried about you and the family," she said. "He's afraid for your lives."

We were back to that again, as if Jim had some vision of danger ahead and was trying to avert it by keeping my family and me in Peoples Temple.

"I really don't care, Marcie. I'm tired of living like this. As far as the idea of brotherhood is concerned, as far as social and economic and racial equality goes—you know I'm totally behind that. I still love my dear old ladies in the nursing homes. But I cannot be a part of this group anymore. I'm sick and tired of being called a daughter when he doesn't even have time to talk to me."

She tried to defend him. "Jim's really busy, you know. And I'm sure that if he knew how he hurt you, he would have talked with you. We love you regardless of what you do, but we're just afraid for your lives if you leave."

"That's fine," I replied. "If all three of us are killed in an explosion, Jim can use it as a warning to the rest of the people. But I'm leaving regardless." It was not as painful as I had feared. I had made my move, and that was it.

At almost the same time, my husband and I decided to call it quits. It was as civil as a breakup can be; I helped him set up his apartment in another part of Ukiah, and he returned to a bachelor's life. My ties with nearly all aspects of the past were cut, and Stephan and I sailed out into the void.

# eleven A SHELTER FOR MARCELINE

FOR THE NEXT THREE and a half years, I became the consummate California divorcée, chasing a whirlwind of money, sex, and adventure. I landed a sales job with a major insurance company and, after a few months, was able to transfer from Ukiah down to Santa Cruz, a medium-sized city on Monterey Bay, on the other side of San Francisco.

Stephan and I eventually moved in with my sales manager, who had four children of his own plus a housekeeper and her child. It was a shaky arrangement, but we stayed together for more than two years nonetheless. I later became a sales manager myself, overseeing the work of fourteen other field representatives. The awards and bonuses that came my way somehow left me cold; although I was working very hard and doing well, my successes failed to touch the emptiness I carried inside. In the front of my insurance manual I jotted a quotation that reflected my feelings: "Succeeding at something you care nothing about is no success at all."

I found more exhilaration when I was in bed with my boyfriend, or parachuting. The thrill of falling backwards off that strut into the blue and then pulling the cord and floating to the ground was a genuine momentary high. Hang-gliding was even greater; I nearly gave my instructor heart failure the first time I launched myself off a cliff and immediately began seeing how high I could soar instead of playing it safe.

My boyfriend and I used to lie in bed on Sunday mornings and mimic the television evangelists. We perfected our mockery until it would have been good enough for a stand-up comedy act. We generally disdained religious people; we'd refer to any person who didn't impress us as "a Christian face." In my spare time I read books on how to destroy people's faith, and would even stop in the middle of selling a life insurance policy to argue with a potential customer who happened to mention God.

My parents returned from Brazil during this time and were heartbroken by what they found when they visited me. I refused to let them pray at meals; my language was shocking. I told my father one day, "I still admire you and I like the results of what you are, but I can't stand the means of how you became that way. I just don't want the name of God mentioned in this house."

The depth of their hurt could be traced all the way back to the circumstances of my birth. A doctor had told my mother that she could not bear children, so my arrival had always been viewed as a special miracle from God. They had been proud when I had followed their steps into missionary service, but in the past few years, their dreams had become nightmares. My mother had received a dream shortly after I went to Peoples Temple that seemed to indicate I would return to my faith at some future point, but the fulfillment of that dream seemed unlikely.

By far a more welcome houseguest in those days was Marceline Jones. Santa Cruz became her "turtle's shell" where she would retreat for three or four days at a time to rest and unwind. We spent long hours together shopping or lying on the beach, digging our toes into the sand and giggling like children. Some people thought she was my sister, and we didn't bother to correct them.

We both enjoyed soul music. One night at my apartment (I retained my own place even though I was living most of the time with my boyfriend), after Stephan was asleep, we put on a Herbie Mann record and danced until at least two-thirty in the morning, letting out all the pent-up frustrations that both of us carried. For a few hours, Jim and Peoples Temple and my career were far away, and we were like mother and daughter back in Belo Horizonte once again, doing a joyful Charleston in the kitchen.

The curtains were open, and we finally collapsed and began laughing at the sight that had greeted any passers-by: two ladies in their housecoats dancing to hot music in the middle of the night.

Jim seemed not to object to Marceline's coming to see me. He apparently realized how therapeutic it was for her. He always called at least once a day, and both of us would talk to him. I got his permission to keep up my contact with my special friends such as Love Life and Ever Rejoicing, even though defectors were not sup-

April 28, 1976

Dearest Bonnie,

Thank you so much for the nice letter you wrote to
the editor of the Chronicle in our behalf.  Jim had
not told them about our time in Brazil .  He said that if
you are contacted about it about the paper to contact
us before replying.  He wasn't at all upset that you mentioned it.
Thought maybe it was a good idea.

I am enclosing an article that I wanted you to have
a copy of.  Jim's Indian ancestry really shows, doesn't it?

Bonnie, I want to thank you again for the beautiful
time you gave me while I was there.  I was so happy
to hear your voice and to know that you are feeling so
much better.

Tell your doctor friend that I have started the
vitamin regimen he suggested for me.  I'll let him know
how it works. If he cures my cough, he will have done something
no one has been able to do and I've tried for years.

Please forgive the typing.  I was writing reprts for
work and decided to type you a note.  I'm certainly glad
I don't have to make a living typing.

I just finished a survey of a convalescent hosp.
where the nursing care is beautiful.  They do exist, rarely.

Give my love to Stephan.  Much love to you, always.

Marcie

posed to be allowed such privileges. He notified his nursing home managers to let my letters and phone calls go through. And I returned the favor by sending occasional checks to help with the old folks' expenses.

Altogether Marceline may have come to visit fifteen or twenty times between 1974 and her departure for Guyana in 1977. She was having physical problems in addition to her emotional stresses, and I encouraged her to see a doctor about her persistent cough. Sometimes she couldn't stop coughing for five minutes at a time. It was eventually diagnosed as lung cancer, even though she was not a smoker; no one at the temple was permitted to smoke or drink. At one point Jim claimed to have healed her, but it was an empty claim.

Thus the warm sunshine of the beach was good for her body as well as her spirit. One day a group of us were fooling around with a paperback on graphology that had four symbols that would allegedly reveal one's personality, depending on the order of preference. I'd already tried it on several of my sales reps, and it had been surprisingly accurate in some cases. I gave it to Marceline, and she made her choices.

According to the book, she came out an absolute maniac for sex. We had an uproarious time teasing her while her face turned red. In fact, she was rather conservative in that area and had always been loyal to Jim, which made things all the funnier.

But late at night, there would be times when I would hear Marceline sobbing in her room. The sexual escapades of her husband were no laughing matter then. I would go in and try to comfort her, but there wasn't a lot that could be said. It was helpful for her just to cry.

A few times I did say, "Marcie, I wish I could get you out of all this. I wish I could just knock you on the head and kidnap you. I know what suffering you're going through, and I really care about you. I love you."

She would smile and return my expressions of love, but she would not criticize her husband. Neither would I, for fear of losing her friendship. One of her daughters had left Peoples Temple and said she hated her father, and Marceline never had anything to do with that daughter again. I knew she continued to love her, but she was trapped.

I made a visit back to Redwood Valley in 1976, staying at the Jones home overnight. Jim was again kind, as he had always been on the phone. We sat in the living room talking, and he said, "I can really see a change in you since you left. You've matured a lot. You've gained a lot of confidence." We stayed away from touchy subjects, until Marceline and I could leave for dinner at a restaurant. I also found time to drive around and see my elderly friends before returning to Santa Cruz.

But the longer the months rolled on, the more I worried about Marceline and what Peoples Temple was becoming. One time she brought her Stephan and his girlfriend, Michelle, and a five-year-old boy from the temple down for a day of fun at Marriott's Great America amusement park just north of San Jose. We had hardly finished breakfast together when the little guy piped up.

"Do you believe in God?"

"No."

"Well, that's good," he announced, "because we cut the penises off capitalists and people who believe in God."

Chills shot up my spine. I thought to myself, "If they're feeding little children that kind of hatred and hostility, how in the world will their values of peace and pacifism and tolerance for all mankind ever get anywhere?"

I do not believe that anyone was ever castrated by Peoples Temple, but the rhetoric alone was dangerous. I found out how vicious it had become when I drove up to

# THE BROKEN GOD

San Francisco to be with the Joneses at the temple there for a special service around New Year's Day, 1977. Marceline decided that for my protection, she and I should enter the service after it had already started, and should leave before it finished.

It was the first time I had been in a Peoples Temple meeting for three years, and I was swept by strange feelings. I wasn't an outsider to the Jones family, but I certainly wasn't an insider as far as these people were concerned. Gene and Phyllis Chaikin passed me by with total disdain. So did a number of others. Only Love Life greeted me with warmth as I kissed her wrinkled face.

Jim was already on the platform when we entered. The choir began its presentation, and I found myself clapping with them and singing along as much as I could remember. A group of teenage boys then put on an impressive Afro-American dance.

But next came a long movie, made in Cuba with English subtitles, about betrayal and fascism. I was bored. Jim considered it very important. "It's getting too late. It's getting too late," he told the crowd. "America is coming into fascism, and so we have no room for traitors. If we find out you're a traitor, we're going to kill you."

Two skits followed that genuinely disturbed me. A white man and woman lived in luxury with black servants, whom they bossed around imperiously. Suddenly, a mob of blacks came rushing in with guns and knives to handcuff the couple, shoot them in the head, and then decapitate them. That was the end of the skit; the audience gave it a standing ovation.

My heart bled for one of the black players, a towering guy named Jim McElvane. I remembered how gentle he had been when he first came to the group, full of love and caring for the elderly. I remembered his touching story one night about finding some doughnuts somewhere and trying to figure out how to get the ants off the doughnuts without harming them. Now here he was, acting out unspeakable violence.

In the second skit, God was portrayed as a simpleton in a dunce's cap wearing a white wig and a long beard, perched up on a ladder. The people below ran around tossing insults in his direction. It was bad drama, but worse than that, it was bad psychology. The fruits of such indoctrination could not be good, I knew, and for the first time I began to worry about what Peoples Temple might do to the world.

# twelve THE NEW BEGINNING

MY "ARRANGEMENT" WITH my boyfriend came crashing to the ground in early 1976, and for a time I dated no one. I threw myself even more into my work. But before long I had bounced to the opposite extreme, dating virtually seven nights a week with seven different men—a marine biologist, an attorney, a dentist, a parapsychologist, a jewelry store owner, a real estate salesman, and I've forgotten what the seventh one did. They all knew about one another, and yet, for the time being, they stuck with "the blond bomber," as I came to be known.

Such madness was only a cover-up for the ache that was mounting inside my spirit. In a way, I was like Marceline, trapped in a life-style that was becoming more and more distasteful all the time. My faith in everything had been destroyed. The neat men, my sportscar, my apartment, my jewelry, my financial stockpile—what did they mean? Nothing at all.

I began dating a sales manager of my company who lived in another part of the Bay Area. In contrast to my earlier relationships, this one began to look as if it could develop into something. As the spring wore on, we began using a word I thought I had left forever: marriage.

But I was not overjoyed at the prospect. How could I know that this time would be any more successful or fulfilling than before? I was attracted to him and thought I would love being his wife, but at the same time, doubts plagued my mind. Could I really believe in this man? I had believed in Jim Jones, and my first husband, and the minister I went to see in southern California back in 1971, and a long list of dates, and in the end been disappointed every time.

My weariness with life continued to grow until, on the evening of May 5, I returned in desperation to the final solution I had attempted once before. I was not an impetuous teenager this time; I was a thirty-one-year-old woman who was sick of living and wanted out. Again, I laid a careful plan. I got a baster from my kitchen, went out to my new MGB convertible, and proceeded to extract as much of the brake fluid as I could. Tomorrow morning I would head up winding, treacherous Highway 1 along the ocean and accelerate around one of the cliffside curves. When they found the car at the bottom of the canyon, they would learn that the brake fluid had somehow leaked away, and nothing more.

Stephan was asleep. I sat in a lounge chair that evening

in my living room all alone. Nervous, I picked up the phone and called my brother, Mark, who was married and living in Mountain View, near San Jose. Something in my voice apparently gave me away; he said, "Stay right where you are, Bonnie—I'll be there in forty minutes."

When he arrived, I didn't tell him of my plan; perhaps I didn't need to. But I did say, "Mark, I just can't stand to live like this anymore. I've got all the material things a person could want, and yet I'm miserable. Life seems entirely in vain."

Mark was very tender with me as he said, "If I could carry the load on your shoulders, I would do it. But that's impossible. The problem is yours." He paused a moment before continuing. "I think I have the answer, but whether or not you're willing to accept it I don't know."

I should have known what he was going to say next, but I didn't.

"Well, what is it?" I asked.

"Do you remember the verse in the Bible that says if you seek God with all your heart, you'll find him? It's somewhere in Jeremiah."

"Yes, I remember." That wasn't the answer I had hoped for, but I kept listening.

He finally said a little prayer for me—which was the first time that had happened in my house for years—and then after about forty minutes he left.

I went to my bedroom and lay face down in the shag carpeting. I began to cry. Hostility, anger, and frustration came bubbling to the surface. After about ten minutes, I decided to try what Mark had said. I was like a person lost in the water at sea with no life raft or help of any kind, and the moon hidden by clouds. I had no reason to believe that there would be anyone to listen, but just in case, I cried out anyway.

I am not proud of the prayer I prayed that night, either

its tone or its language. In my insolence, I felt that God—if he were there—had some pretty big explaining to do to me, not only about the state of the world in general but also why my life had turned out the way it had. So I said:

"OK, you s.o.b.—if you're really up there, and if what Mark said was really from you, I'm willing to seek you harder than anyone else in the world has ever done. I'm willing to go farther to find you than anyone has ever gone." That was all. I waited in silence.

Amazingly, God didn't strike me dead for my vulgarity, and he apparently brushed off my belligerence as well. A peace seemed to settle over me, and after a while I sat up on the floor.

The thought came to me to read something. I had long since thrown out all my Bibles and religious books, but I had kept one little devotional classic, A. J. Russell's *God at Eventide*, for its sentimental value. It had been a gift at the death of Stephany. I rummaged through the bookshelves until I found it, and since it was already past midnight now, I turned to the meditation for May 6.

I could hardly believe my eyes.

> *Seek and you shall find.*
>
> *As a mother hiding from her child puts herself in the way of being found, so with Me. So the finding of Me and of the treasures of My Kingdom may not always depend upon ardent intent securing attainment, but upon the mere setting out on the quest.*
>
> *Is this a comfort to you?*
>
> *When you set out upon a time of seeking I place Myself in your way, and the sometime arid path of prayer becomes a fertile glade in which you are surprised to find your search so soon over. Thus mutual Joy.*

# THE BROKEN GOD

I was astounded. Just a few minutes ago, I had become the little child, seeking for God, and he had immediately responded that I didn't have to go two thousand miles to find him; the first step was enough.

None of my questions had been answered. I still didn't know why my daughter had died, or why so many Christians were such bigots, or why the minister had propositioned me, or why I had had to go through the whole Peoples Temple nightmare. But I couldn't have felt more consoled. It was as if a big voice had come booming through the bedroom ceiling to say, "This is God, honey—don't be afraid. I love you." I simply knew that there was a God after all, and he had spoken to me.

Mark and his wife, Darlene, were back on Saturday, and they gently suggested that I needed to get back to the Scriptures and also to receive the teaching of an established church. The second part frightened me; I would much preferred to have stayed one-to-one with God and avoided all those hypocrites. But I agreed nevertheless to go with them the next day to Bethel Church in San Jose, where they worshiped. It wasn't as bad as I had feared. I did sense that God was in this place.

And over the next few weeks and months, I began to see signs that God was perhaps alive and interested in me after all. The Scriptures began to make sense again. I began to feel uncomfortable about my relationship with the other sales manager, whose divorce had not yet even been finalized. I met him for lunch and told him it was over. Within four days I stumbled onto the information that he'd been carrying on an affair with one of his sales reps all the while he'd been talking marriage with me. He eventually dubbed me "Virgin Mary" because of my new set of values.

The other men I had dated in the early part of the year were a bit incredulous at first. I casually explained that my highs weren't coming in night clubs now and weren't subject to hangovers. I was still the same person with many of the same problems, but the peace inside was making a great difference.

The person I most wanted to talk to about all this was Marceline, and yet at the same time I was afraid. She and Jim had moved to San Francisco by now, where he relished his post as chairman of the housing authority (thanks to the support Peoples Temple had given George Moscone in the last mayoral election). But at the same time Jim's paranoia was growing as defectors became more vocal.

I drove up to visit Marceline just as the famous expose appeared in *New West* magazine at the beginning of August, 1977. It was the last time I would ever see her. She was staying in a small room in the temple with another woman named Sandy Bradshaw. "Jim's gone to Guyana until things blow over," Marcie explained.

She gave me a large manila envelope that morning with copies of *New West* and the other accusations that had recently appeared. I didn't take time to read them then; only after I returned home did I study them and realize that they were 98 percent true. She told me that Grace Stoen had defected and that now there would be a custody battle over five-year-old John-John, her son whom Jim claimed to have fathered at Tim Stoen's request. Tim and Grace were determined to get the boy back.

I could sense a reluctance in Marceline; she wanted me to know how critical things were, but she didn't want to have to verbalize it. So she gave me the clippings instead. We then turned to happier topics.

She told me about Jonestown, the new paradise being built in Guyana, and showed me pictures of its progress. Soon we went to a nearby restaurant, the Copper Penny, and I hoped that now I could talk openly with her about spiritual things, since Sandy was not along. I was anxious to find the right time and place to say, "Marcie, I still believe in helping and loving people and doing the best we can—but there's also a peace on the inside that you can find in God that will far outweigh what you have through what you call 'truth.' I think I've found a way to help you cope with all the pain and fear you're carrying inside."

The restaurant proved to be a frustration. Too many people kept recognizing Mrs. Jim Jones and coming up to talk. Time was slipping away, and I had a deadline by which I had to be back in San Jose.

We stopped on the way back from lunch to see Love Life, who had been moved to San Francisco as well. I was concerned about the old woman, because my phone calls to her in recent weeks had not seemed natural. She had a peculiar greeting she always used with everyone—the single word "Peace." But she stretched it out, her voice starting low and scooping up at the end; it was her trademark.

I walked into her room, bent down, and kissed her, and she responded with "Peeeeace—is that you, Bonnie?"

"Yes, Love Life, it's me. How are you?"

But just as in the phone calls, she wouldn't say much. She knew better than to talk with other people in the room. We left after a few minutes and returned to Marcie's cubicle.

We began looking through old scrapbooks together. For some reason, Marceline felt like talking about her Stephany. We looked at pictures of how she looked when she first arrived from Korea, covered with lice and scabs. Marceline told how upset the girl had become when Jim took his first out-of-town trip, and how Jim had calmed her over the telephone.

Then we came to the page of Stephany's funeral in 1959. Below the picture, Marceline had written, "Dear God, help me to bear this terrible burden." I made a note of that in my mind; it was proof that at one point this troubled woman had known and loved the God who had become real to me so recently.

Marceline launched into the story of how she had spanked Stephany for stepping on ants the Saturday before the car accident on Sunday, and how guilty she still felt about that. I nervously glanced at the clock as she talked on and eventually realized that I wasn't going to get to share the purpose of my coming after all.

I said goodbye, and when I got home, I wrote her a long, long letter the next day, saying all the things I had wanted to say in person. I never got an answer, and I never saw Marceline again.

Neither did I ever see Love Life again. When I called the next week, I was informed that she had been moved to Jonestown. I was furious and called Marceline.

"Where's Love Life?" I demanded.

"She was sent on down to paradise."

"Do you mean to tell me," I stormed, "that they took a woman who's been like my own mother without letting her even call me to say goodbye?"

"Well, Bonnie," she said, "you know, we're fleeing the country, and we couldn't take a chance that someone would know what we're doing. I'll tell you what I'll do. I'm going to Guyana next week. Write Love Life a letter, and I'll carry it to her."

I prepared a sentimental letter, complete with a lock of my hair, and forwarded it to Marceline. I eventually received a reply, but it obviously was not from Love Life. I didn't expect it to be in her handwriting, of course, since her glaucoma had always forced her to dictate her letters to someone else. But I knew her well enough to know whether she was behind the dictation or not. This letter had none of the warmth and tenderness of Love Life. There was no "Peace" at the beginning. It was a patchwork of what I called "J.J.'s cliches"—flowery descriptions of Jonestown and how it was the most wonderful place she'd ever hoped to see.

I tore it up in a rage, and I knew that all was not well in the Guyana jungle.

# thirteen ONE LAST ATTEMPT

FIFTEEN MONTHS AFTER MY LAST MEETING with Marceline, I was in the midst of entertaining guests on a Saturday night when the telephone interrupted.

"My name is Ross Case, and I live up in Ukiah," the voice said. I was busy fixing dinner and didn't especially want to be bothered. The name meant nothing to me.

He explained that he had been Jim's assistant back in the 1950s, pastoring Peoples Temple in Indianapolis while the Joneses went to Brazil. He and his wife, Louella, had been among the vanguard that came out to northern California to find a new place safe from atomic danger.

But Ross had begun to get bad vibrations from friends back in Indianapolis who wrote him, and when he confirmed that Jim was indeed denying God, Jesus Christ, and the Bible, he had dropped out of the group.

"My question is," he went on, "would you be willing to join a delegation of concerned relatives who are going down to Guyana with Congressman Leo Ryan the week after next? Some of those people are being held prisoner down there; they can't leave, and their relatives can't get in to see them. Debbie Layton Blakey got out a few months ago and told the State Department all about what's going on, but they wouldn't believe her. Now Ryan is going to check it out. And if anybody can talk sense to Jim, it's you."

We must have talked for forty-five minutes while my meal overcooked and my guests waited downstairs. "Mr. Case," I said, "I know what you're talking about; I'm really worried too about whatever is going on in Jonestown. But I don't want to do anything hasty."

I then went on to explain why I especially didn't want to leave home right now. Over the past year, I had met and married the most gracious, understanding Christian man I could ever dream of. We had first gotten acquainted at Bethel Church not long after I began attending there; his name was Hank Thielmann, and he was in construction. He had been through a difficult divorce himself, and so we took our time getting to know one another. He treated me like a virgin, and I, with the Lord's help, even managed to behave like one. I was disturbed for a while about whether the Bible allowed for remarriage. But after some fasting, prayer, and study, I came to the belief that God did not penalize those who ruined his plan of wedlock by demanding lifelong celibacy ever after. When Hank and I were married after a year of dating, Stephan had a father again, and I started a whole new life of joyous companionship.

"I'm a newlywed of five months," I told Ross Case, "and I've never been happier in my life. I'm not really anxious to go chasing off to South America on a dangerous mission. Hank and I will have to talk and pray about it, and why don't you call me back around next Wednesday?"

"I'll do that, Bonnie," he replied, "and I'll also talk to some friends who might be willing to put up the money for your ticket. I just believe that you especially need to be along on that trip for whatever purposes God might want to use you."

The implications began hitting me almost as soon as I hung up the phone. I came down the stairs speechless; I slumped into a chair and let out a loud groan from deep within that Hank described later as the most horrible cry he'd ever heard. I told my guests what had just transpired, and we talked of little else over dinner.

After they left, and after Hank went on to sleep, I stayed up to think and pray. "Lord," I said, "I really need to know from you what I should do in this circumstance. I really can't make this decision by myself."

I began turning the pages of my Living Bible and stopped at Psalm 107. Verse 2 seemed to relate to my situation:

> *Has the Lord redeemed you? Then speak out! Tell others he has saved you from your enemies.*

A few pages back, I came across an even more pointed section:

> *Lord, how long shall the wicked be allowed to triumph and exult? Hear their insolence! See their arrogance! How these men of evil boast! See them oppressing your people, O*

> *Lord, afflicting those you love. They murder widows,*
> *immigrants, and orphans, for "The Lord isn't looking,"*
> *they say, "and besides, he doesn't care."*
>
> *Fools! Is God deaf and blind—he who makes ears and*
> *eyes? He punishes the nations—won't he also punish you?*
> *He knows everything—doesn't he also know what you are*
> *doing? (Ps. 94:3-10)*

I leaned back and closed my eyes, thinking about how perfectly the passage described Jim Jones.

But then a little further down the column, the words seemed to relate directly to me.

> *Who will protect me from the wicked? Who will be my*
> *shield? I would have died unless the Lord had helped me. I*
> *screamed, "I'm slipping, Lord!" and he was kind and saved*
> *me.*
>
> *. . . Will you permit a corrupt government to rule under*
> *your protection—a government permitting wrong to defeat*
> *right? Do you approve of those who condemn the innocent*
> *to death? No! The Lord my God is my fortress—the mighty*
> *Rock where I can hide. God has made the sins of evil men to*
> *boomerang upon them! He will destroy them by their own*
> *plans. Jehovah our God will cut them off. (vv. 16-18,*
> *20-23)*

One more Scripture seemed to speak to me that night, from Isaiah 49:24-26:

> *Who can snatch the prey from the hands of a mighty*
> *man? Who can demand that a tyrant let his captives go?*
> *But the Lord says, "Even the captives of the most mighty*
> *and the most terrible shall all be freed; for I will fight those*
> *who fight you, and I will save your children. I will feed your*
> *enemies with their own flesh and they shall be drunk with*

*rivers of their own blood. All the world shall know that I,
the Lord, am your Savior and Redeemer, the Mighty One of
Israel.*

I interpreted that passage to mean that the Ryan mission
would be successful. Perhaps I really did belong in
Guyana, helping to bring about the release of the captives.

It was too big a decision to make in one night, but I
went to sleep optimistic. The timing was convenient; I
had recently left the insurance company and was now
studying to become a realtor. I could get away for a week
with no problem. Hank and I continued to talk over the
next few days, and I continued to search the Scriptures
for guidance.

Ross Case called back on Wednesday, November 8, as
planned, and we must have talked for two hours. As he
told what he had been finding out, I had to face the
painful fact that Marceline was not as blind to the realities
of Peoples Temple as I had always hoped. She was definitely a part of what Jim was doing, although at that time
I didn't know the full extent of the pressures to cooperate
that he had brought to bear upon her.

Ross told me the names of two donors who would help
buy my ticket. He assured me of his prayers and offered
to let me use his home if at any point I needed a place to
get away or to hide.

When Hank got home, we sat down together to make
up our minds. "Father," we prayed, "we know that this
could be a very dangerous mission. We're deeply in love;
we don't want to be apart; we'd like to play it safe. But if
it's your will for me to go to Guyana, please fulfill the
following conditions." I wrote them down in my
notebook.

1.  Expenses must be paid before leaving.

2. The congressman and the district attorney must consent to my going.

3. Travel documents must come through in time—passport, visa, medical okays, etc.

Any hitch on any of the three counts would rule out the trip.

Ross called back early the next morning to say I could pick up the $1,200 on Saturday. He also mentioned that Tim Stoen, formerly an attorney for Peoples Temple but now in private practice in the Bay Area and the organizer of the concerned-relatives group, would be calling me.

As we talked, Tim said, "I really feel you should go with us. I'll call Leo Ryan and recommend that you be added to the list." By the afternoon, conditions one and two had been met.

I called the passport office in Santa Cruz, who told me there was no chance of getting a passport in time, short of driving to the agency in San Francisco. It was too late on Thursday for that, and the next day was Veterans Day, after which came the weekend. If I were to get a passport, it would have to be gotten all in a single day—next Monday—before the group flew out that night. The chances seemed slim.

I returned to the Scriptures that day, and again certain passages seemed to jump out at me, but they were not so reassuring as before. Isaiah 47: 8-11 read:

> You say, "I alone am God! I'll never be a widow; I'll never lose my children." Well, those two things shall come upon you in one moment, in full measure in one day: widowhood and the loss of your children, despite all your witchcraft and magic.
>
> You felt secure in all your wickedness. "No one sees me," you said. Your "wisdom" and "knowledge" have caused you to turn away from me and claim that you yourself are

*Jehovah. That is why disaster shall overtake you suddenly—so suddenly that you won't know where it comes from. And there will be no atonement then to cleanse away your sins."*

By Friday the picture looked even worse:

*Therefore the Lord God says: I will destroy you for these "visions" and lies. My hand shall be against you, and you shall be cut off from among the leaders of Israel; I will blot out your names and you will never see your own country again. And you shall know I am the Lord. (Ezek. 13:8-9)*

Something sank within me as I read those verses. I knew in my spirit that God was telling me Jim Jones would never come back to the United States alive. I desperately clung to the hope of the final verse of the chapter:

*But you will lie no more; no longer will you talk of seeing "visions" that you never saw, nor practice your magic, for I will deliver my people out of your hands by destroying you, and you shall know I am the Lord.*

Then came the bleakest prophecy of all, after which I wanted to read no more. It came from the obscure book of Zephaniah:

*I will make you as helpless as a blind man searching for a path, because you have sinned against the Lord; therefore your blood will be poured out into the dust and your bodies will lie there rotting on the ground. (1:17)*

Surely it was an exaggeration.

On Saturday we drove to Ukiah to meet Ross Case and

119

the donors. I was overcome with their generosity. Early Sunday morning, I wrote out a simple will, which I had witnessed by the couple who taught our Sunday school class. The pastor's sermon that morning emphasized that Christians have no right to sit back and relax, avoiding involvement in the world around us. It seemed almost like a plot.

By Sunday night, I was coming down to the wire, and both Hank and I could feel the tension mounting. We stayed home from church that night. It was one of the most bittersweet evenings of my life. He couldn't verbalize what he was feeling inside, but he began trying to take pictures of me with his Polaroid. The camera wouldn't produce, and he gave up. I crawled into bed and he sat down beside me on the floor for a long talk.

"Honey, the reason you were trying to take those pictures is because you're afraid I'm not coming back, isn't it?"

He nodded.

"Sweetheart," I continued, "if this really is the end, I want you to know that these five months have been the most beautiful months of my whole life." I went on to urge him to remarry if anything did happen to me.

We talked about what could happen in Guyana. I described my determination to see Jim and Marceline, even to the point of flying to Port Kaituma and walking the last six miles to Jonestown if that became necessary. I had nothing to hide or be ashamed of. I intended to walk right up to the gate, present the letters from Jim and Marceline that welcomed me to visit anytime, and talk my way past the guards. Ross Case had also given me copies of Peoples Temple propaganda that said, "Our community in Guyana is an open book.... As many as 30 visitors, guests from Guyana and from around the world, visit the community everyday." I intended to be one of them.

120

"Hank, do you think I'm being foolish?" I asked.

He took a deep breath and then said, "No, I don't. I really believe you are supposed to go, and God will guide you once you get there."

After a moment he said, "Tell me again what you will say to Jim when you see him."

"I'm going to say, 'Jim, I still really love you—that's why I came down. But look what you're doing to these people. What are you gaining by all this? If a few people want to leave, what will it hurt? You let me leave Peoples Temple, and it didn't harm a thing.'"

I talked about my deep desire to see Love Life once again, and to talk to Marcie and the children, and to help get John-John Stoen out. We closed our talk that night by raising one last danger: the possibility of my being raped.

"Yes, I know there's that chance," Hank said quietly, "but if it happens, I still want you back. Nothing will change in my eyes about you."

The next morning I was up before daylight to finish packing my suitcase and head for the passport agency in San Francisco. I was the second person in line when the doors opened at eight-thirty. I cringed as the first man was scolded for having the gall to want a passport in two days. When my turn came, the clerk took one look at the date of departure I had written on my form and looked up with a scowl.

"What's this?"

"It's an emergency," I explained. "You've been closed for a three-day weekend, and I was told to come here the first thing this morning. I'm going down to Jonestown in Guyana with Leo Ryan."

Suddenly his attitude changed. "Oh, I know about that. Come back at three o'clock."

I breathed a prayer of thanksgiving as I walked out. Condition number three had just been met.

# THE BROKEN GOD

I spent the rest of the day running legal errands for Tim Stoen so that John-John's custody papers would be in order. The Stoens and I had not been extremely close during our Redwood Valley days, but we soon found a common bond now as we talked about the upcoming trip.

"Man, your husband's got to be some guy to let you go off after just five months on a chase like this," Tim remarked.

"He really is," I said with a glow.

"It makes me feel good to hear a wife talk about her husband like that," he added.

A few hours later, Tim and the rest of the group got to meet both Hank and Stephan at the San Francisco airport before we boarded. There were thirteen relatives in the group, plus the press: Don Harris, Bob Brown, Steve Sung, and Bob Flick of NBC, Tim Reiterman and Greg Robinson of the *San Francisco Examiner,* and Ron Javers of the *San Francisco Chronicle.* Charles Krause of the *Washington Post* would join us later. At 10:00 P.M. we lifted off for the overnight flight to New York, where we would meet the congressman and his aides and proceed to our date with the unknown.

# fourteen THE VIGIL

THE NINE-HOUR LAYOVER in New York after a night on the plane left me fatigued with yet another long flight to go. We caught a little sleep in a nearby Holiday Inn before it was time to board Pan American's 3:00 P.M. departure for Georgetown.

I sat in the waiting room and began jotting in my notebook.

> *I see the strain building on people's faces. Mrs. Houston* [wife of Sam Houston, the AP photographer who first brought Peoples Temple to Leo Ryan's attention] *is crying gently. My heart reaches out to all these hurting people who only ask that their loved ones be returned to them.*

123

> *I've tried three times to call Marcie's parents, all to no effect. I'm sitting on the railing just looking at different people. Tim is sitting quietly with his hands in his lap. Grace is sitting next to him. . . . I continue asking myself how this nightmare ever reached these proportions. How blind we all were to the insidious progression of events. . . . I look at the Olivers' faces, Bev and Howard—they're tight with tension. I know all the relatives' hearts are hopeful; yet I realize they must steel themselves against what past experience tells them is inevitable disappointment. . . . If ever I see a miracle, this will be it.*

It would be another twelve hours before I would finally get to a bed. My first several days in Georgetown were an unbroken string of frustrations and delays, starting as soon as we walked into the Pegasus Hotel at about three o'clock Wednesday morning, Guyana time.

"We never received your reservations," the desk clerk said in his British accent. "I am sorry, but the hotel is full; all 109 rooms are taken."

"Why so much business on an ordinary November night?" I demanded.

"We have three conferences here all at once."

I was immediately suspicious and asked to see the guest list. He would not show it to me, but eventually I wheedled him into giving in, after promising to keep still about it. There were indeed 109 names on the roster—one of which was "Mr. and Mrs. J. Jones." That gave further credibility to my theory that Peoples Temple had bought out the hotel that night in advance of our coming.

Some of us eventually took a taxi to the Towers, another hotel nearby, where for twenty-seven dollars I got a room with no hot water and woefully weak air conditioning. The mattress sagged while the cockroaches ran underneath, but the jungle birds that sang outside—even at four in the morning—lent some charm to the situation.

The more serious frustrations had to do with the American embassy. While I had determined to deal directly with Peoples Temple, Leo and the others tried to make arrangements through the ambassador and his staff. Leo's very coming was in some ways an indictment of their earlier responses to State Department requests for information; they'd been out to Jonestown several times and pronounced it acceptable. No laws were being broken so far as they were concerned. But now a congressman had come to see for himself.

The attempted dinner at the ambassador's swank home that Wednesday night was a waste of time from my perspective, since it was obvious that he was not interested in hearing my story or Jim Cobb's. Even Leo was becoming upset by then. Ambassador Burke had already dodged some of his questions by citing the Privacy Act of 1974, and Leo told the two of us that night, "I am really teed off. I'm down here as a member of the House International Affairs Committee, doing a congressional investigation, and I'm getting only the most meager cooperation." He asked if Jim Cobb and I would be willing to testify in a congressional hearing on the matter, and we both said yes.

With the press, of course, Leo continued to sound neutral and dispassionate so as not to jeopardize his image with anyone, but underneath, we knew what he was feeling.

The next afternoon at two o'clock, our entire group went to the embassy for a conference. John Burke could afford only one hour to see us, we were told, and he insisted that the newsmen stay outside. We were ushered upstairs to his office, where chairs had been set up theater-style before a large screen. Part of our hour was going to be chewed up with a slide show of Jonestown.

We could tell by the pictures that Jim and the commune had staged quite an exhibition for the diplomats with their cameras. I caught one glimpse of Marceline, but basically, the slides didn't tell us anything we didn't already know. When they were finished, we moved our chairs into a semicircle and began, one by one, to tell the ambassador and his two assistants our stories.

Steve Katsaris began, describing his earlier visit to Jonestown during which he was not allowed to speak to Maria, his daughter, alone. Howard and Beverly Oliver told about their earlier trip as well, trying to regain their two sons, one of whom was only seventeen. Howard began to weep, and so Beverly finished for him.

Tim Stoen discussed some of our legal rights to see our children and other relatives. Then Jim Cobb spoke, and Wayne Pietila, and then I told about living with the Joneses, the death threats when I left the temple, and the suicide pacts I knew had been formed.

Next came Mickey Touchette, who told of the agony her family members inside Peoples Temple put her through once she left. Her story had the rest of us in tears—even Tim, Howard, and Leo Ryan. Meanwhile, John Burke sat completely stonefaced, toying with something in his hands; I believe it was a cigar. Not a flicker of emotion showed in his eyes.

When we were finished, he proceeded to hand us photocopies of the following statement, written the day before.

### PRESS STATEMENT

*The People's Temple Community at Jonestown is a group of private American citizens who have chosen to come to Guyana as permanent or semi-permanent residents. As with private American citizens residing anywhere abroad, they are subject to the laws and regulations of the host country, in this case Guyana. The American Embassy in Georgetown has no official contact with the People's Temple other than the provision of normal consular services to the individual members of this community on a regular basis. These services include renewal of passports, registration of births, etc. The Embassy has no official authority over the community or its individual members. Except as provided for in the Vienna Convention on Consular Relations and in the Bilateral Consular Convention that is in force between our two countries, the Embassy does not have any legal right to demand access to any private American citizen in Guyana. In light of this, the Embassy has no authority to require contacts between members of the People's Temple and persons whom they do not wish to receive. The members of the People's Temple are protected by the Privacy Act of 1974, as are all American citizens.*

*11/15/78.*

We were totally at wit's end. We told him that in our trips out to Lamaha Gardens, Linda Amos had said, "If you want to see your families, go to the embassy." After pleading, the ambassador finally did go to the phone and call Lamaha to say, "I would appreciate it and consider it a personal favor if you would allow the relatives to see their loved ones. It seems to me that, after all your claims of persecution, you could strengthen your position considerably simply by letting these people in and then sending them on their way." It was the one small assistance we received from him.

By the time I got back to the hotel that afternoon, I was discouraged. The Guyanese water had combined with

THE BROKEN GOD

the frustrations of bureaucracy to make me miserable. At that low point, something nice finally happened. I felt an arm around my shoulders and turned around to see Leo Ryan, who had just walked into the hotel lobby.

"You look like you could use some rest," he said. "Why don't we sit down and talk for a while?"

We went upstairs to suite 504, which had become the press room for our group. It happened to be empty. I was still choked up from the afternoon at the embassy, and he said softly, "Try to bear up. The end is coming soon. Everything's going to be all right. We're going to get the people out."

We sat down. "Bonnie," he said, putting his feet up on a coffee table, "I don't think I've met a woman anything like you. You're by far the gutsiest woman I've ever known. I don't know how you could go through all you've gone through and still care so much about people."

I tried not to show my embarrassment. He went on.

"You know, as a congressman there are some things you don't exactly advertise, but I can feel free to say this to you: it's obvious to me that you have a deep faith in God. I'd really like for you to tell me about that."

I laughed. "Listen, you better be careful what you ask me. I might get halfway through, and you'll be sorry."

"No, no, I'm serious. Tell me how you got out of Peoples Temple and got back to your faith in God again."

I started into my story. I told him about the doubts Jim had planted in my mind as a teenager about the existence of God in such an evil world.

"That's a very valid question," he cut in. "What's the answer?"

"Well, I'm not sure God has given me all the answers down pat. But I can tell you how I've come to resolve it for myself." I gave him the illustration of the time Stephan, at the age of nine, had stolen a toy car from a dime store. I told how humiliated I had felt, answering the questions of the police and the store owner. But I had realized that, in spite of my desires as a mother, he had a volition of his own to choose right or wrong. And he, like mankind in general, had chosen the wrong.

"God loves us all," I concluded. "He doesn't always love the things we do, but the point remains that God—unlike many preachers, and unlike Jim Jones—is a gentleman; he doesn't push himself on anyone. We have the choice of whether or not to turn his way."

"That sounds reasonable," Leo responded.

We talked of other things, and finally he said, "Well, Bonnie, when it comes my time to face Saint Peter, I can see him coming out with this big legal-sized ledger and saying, 'OK, Ryan, what about this, and this, and this?'

"And I'll say, 'You're right, Saint Peter. I blew it.' But then I'll say, 'Now let's draw a line down the middle of your pad there, and I'll tell you some of the good things I did, the ways I helped people, and so forth.' And when we're done, I think the ledger is going to be balanced."

I didn't bother to comment on whether that was orthodox theology, but I was impressed by the warmth, the openness, the humility, and the good will of this man. About that time, Jim Schollert and Jackie Speier, two members of his staff, came in. It was time to get ready for the eight o'clock dinner he was hosting that evening for all of us in the group. I went to my room and promptly fell asleep. When I didn't show up by eight-fifteen, he sent Mickey Touchette to awaken me. It was a delicious meal, and after some informal talking, I excused myself and returned to bed.

The next morning, which was Friday, I busied myself with trying to crack through to Guyanese politicians. Our phone calls and visits to Prime Minister Forbes Burnham's office were being brushed aside, but I did manage to speak with a member of Parliament. He suggested I see the deputy commissioner of police, Cecil Glasgow. Tim Stoen, Howard Oliver, and I left to see him just as the congressman and his party were leaving for Jonestown that afternoon. Our hearts were headed for the airport, but our bodies went instead to the deputy commissioner's office.

"Leo Ryan and the group are now on their way," we told him. "Is it at all possible for some armed policemen to accompany them? There is going to be bloodshed. Lives are going to be lost if you do not help."

He leaned back in his chair, began to smile—and then laughed at what he felt was a blatant exaggeration. I fought to keep from lashing out; I wanted to call him a Pontius Pilate and several other things, but I settled for a simple question.

'Is that funny to you?"

He didn't answer me directly, and we returned to the Pegasus to wait.

I passed some time that afternoon in the hotel pool, where I met a young Guyanese girl who told me about her encounter with Jim Jones. She had gone to a meeting at a Georgetown Catholic church at which Jim tried to perform the most amazing healings.

"There was an attorney who had come down here from the States with him, who had been in a wheelchair for many years. His wife pushed him into the meeting. The other healings that night didn't seem believable to me" (apparently Jim was out of practice), "but when he said something to this man, he jumped up and began walking all around the church! It was fantastic."

Something clicked in my mind, and I said, "Would you recognize the attorney's name if I said it?"

"It was kind of an unusual name."

"Eugene Chaikin?"

"That's it—that's the one!" she cried.

I began laughing so hard I could hardly explain to her that I had once worked for the man, and he'd never been paralyzed a day in his life.

I later met the embarrassed Jesuit, Father Morrison, who had allowed Jim into his church. He told me the same story, unsolicited, and again I told what a hoax it was.

It was late Friday evening that the go-ahead came through from Linda Amos for me to go to Jonestown at Jim's invitation. When Leo radioed his strange refusal the next morning, it plunged me into another siege of waiting and wondering. I was now into my fourth day in Guyana, and my chances of getting to Jim and Marceline were lower than ever.

At the same time I felt that if I could just be there with Leo and the others, I could possibly defuse whatever was going wrong.

Most of us were sitting in the lobby waiting at three o'clock that afternoon, the time at which Leo was to be back for an appointment with the prime minister. The hour came and went, and finally Tim Stoen was informed by the Guyana police that the plane would not be back until five. No reason was given for the delay.

We waited. When five o'clock came, the arrival time was pushed back to seven. Nine extra people were coming back with Leo. Who they were wasn't clear. We knew that if darkness fell, planes would be stranded overnight at the Port Kaituma airstrip for lack of lighting.

I returned to my room with Father Morrison, and we began talking. Suddenly, the telephone rang.

"Hello—is Bonnie there?"

"This is Bonnie."

"This is Jimmy."

"Jimmy who?"

"Jimmy Jones."

I squealed with surprise. "Oh, Jimmy, where are you?"

"Down in the lobby."

I tore down four flights of stairs and rushed into the arms of this lanky, bearded young man whose diapers I had changed as a baby back in Brazil. I began crying, until finally he said in his deep voice, "Bonnie . . . everybody's looking at us."

Indeed they were; Guyanese don't often see weepy blonds rushing into the embrace of big black men. We moved around behind one of the large plants in the lobby.

"Oh, Jimmy, I'm sorry I embarrassed you, but it's been so long—I just want to make sure you're OK. How are you really?"

"Man, I'm really happy," he answered with a grin. "I just turned eighteen, I just got married, and I'm on the basketball team."

We talked about his new wife for a moment before I asked, "Jimmy, are you really happy?"

"No, I can't wait to get home," he **said**. My heart skipped a beat. Had he defected?

"I can't wait to get back to Jonestown and see my wife."

I swallowed my disappointment and went on. "Jimmy, I came to visit you and your folks; I'm not an enemy—I love all you guys."

"Well, Bonnie," he said, growing more serious, "if you'd come alone, we'd have had you out to Jonestown right away. But because of when and how you came, it's been a different story."

"All the relatives want is to see their loved ones, which isn't really too much to ask."

About that time, Tim Jones came up; he had been adopted into the family later on, and so I knew him less than the others. A teenager named Mark Cordell was with him, and he greeted me warmly.

Then I spotted Stephan Jones. In contrast with the others, he looked ghastly. His cheeks were sunk in and he had a glassy look in his eyes. I wasn't sure where I stood with him anymore. I approached him cautiously.

"Steve, I'm Bonnie."

"I know who you are," he said, reaching over to hug me and give me a kiss. That took me by surprise, and I began to cry again.

"Steve, I'm here just because I'm concerned about you all. You're like my own family, you know; I named my son after you."

"I know that. I'm just sorry you came at this time." He seemed to soften for a moment, to step out of his lifelong role as a tough guy.

I told him I thought he didn't look well, and he blamed it on the rigorous basketball practicing he and the Peoples Temple team had been doing. That didn't add up; the other players in the lobby looked fine.

"How are your folks?" I asked.

"Mom's fine, but dad's gone off the beam," he said. "I finally convinced him to let the relatives in, but I'm worried."

There was no way Stephan could have known the horror being enacted in the Jonestown pavilion at that very moment; radio contact at Lamaha Gardens had been lost in the late afternoon. Still, Stephan knew somehow that a disaster was imminent.

And then the boys said they had to leave. They trooped out into the night.

It was eight o'clock. The hotel manager said he wanted to speak with each of us one by one in his office, where two police officers sat. He finally gave the message instead to Steve Katsaris, spokesman for the group: Ryan's plane was not going to return that evening. Something had happened, and our lives might be in danger. They wanted us to go upstairs to one room and be under police guard.

I hadn't eaten since breakfast, and I was a little put out that all of officialdom, which hadn't taken our warnings seriously up to now, suddenly wanted to lock us up. In the end, though, we crowded into room 403, which was Steve's—the ten of us plus one reporter who hadn't gotten to go to Jonestown. Armed guards stood outside the door, and from the window we could see more guards with dogs around the perimeter of the hotel.

We sat through two hours of suspense. At ten o'clock the hotel manager called for Sherwin Harris, the exhusband of Linda Amos, who had come to Guyana to see their daughter, Liane. When Sherwin and the manager didn't return, Steve Katsaris left to join them. He returned with the kind of news we had feared:

"We understand that one person has been shot."

No one fell apart at that; everyone stayed in control. A few minutes later the hotel manager came in.

"Leo Ryan and two of the NBC men have been shot, and we think all three are dead."

I stared at the floor in shock. *Oh, God,* I prayed, *please just let them be wounded.* And then I began to think that if a congressman and two reporters had been shot, all of Jonestown could blow up at any minute, given the instability of Jim Jones' mind.

Steve Katsaris had one more blow to deliver.

"You've all taken this well," he said. "There's something else. Linda Amos, Liane, Christa, and Martin were found murdered this evening at Lamaha Gardens."

So that was why Sherwin Harris had been called from the room. My heart ached for him. He had spent the day at Lamaha Gardens; he had eaten dinner with them no more than three hours ago. He had promised to return tomorrow.

"They were found with their throats slit," Steve added in conclusion.

My stomach began to heave. Who had killed them? Had Linda attacked the children herself, and then committed suicide? Unanswerable questions collided with one another inside my head.

We called Ambassador John Burke's number and spoke with one of his assistants. "How many people have been arrested at Lamaha Gardens?" we asked.

"Twenty."

That left another twenty or thirty who might be looking for us. "Can you please tell us which ones are in custody so we'll know if the dangerous ones are on the loose?"

The assistant refused. It would violate the Privacy Act, she said. We ground our teeth in disgust.

So we began digging for information through stateside sources. Shortly after midnight we got through to Jeannie Mills at the Human Freedom Center in Berkeley, California, a halfway house for cult defectors. It was she who finally confirmed that Leo Ryan and four others were dead on the Port Kaituma airstrip, while thirteen others were wounded.

The reaction of the group in room 403 was a sight I will never forget. I made the following notes in my journal:

> *Everybody's holding up well. Grace and Tim are holding onto each other, wondering if John is still alive. Nadyne Houston is wondering about Carol and her two grandchildren, crying gently. Clare Bouquette is using her rosary. Mickey is pacing back and forth saying, "Now if you feel you're going to go hysterical, tell someone." She wants to*

*make plans to shove mattresses against the door in case they knock off the guard.*

*Howard Oliver sits very controlled. Beverly and his two sons may now be dead. Steve Katsaris sits and then paces Anthony and Maria may both be dead—two beautiful young people.*

*I wonder about Marcie, Love Life, John, all the children and people we love so much.*

*2:05 A.M. A lot of touching is going on—everyone telling the others how brave they are—touching, caring.*

Finally, at around three in the morning, we realized that no more news would be forthcoming until dawn, when Guyanese police could go into Jonestown. Neither could we tell whether our own lives were in actual danger or not. We dispersed to our rooms to try to sleep.

# fifteen GOING HOME

IT WAS RAINING when we awakened on Sunday morning. We regrouped in Steve Katsaris' room and another room nearby, where Sherwin Harris still lay in bed drifting in and out of shock. I knelt beside him and held his hand, praying for help once he awakened to the fact that his daughter was dead.

He squeezed my left hand periodically so hard that my wedding ring bit into the flesh. Then he trembled. His eyes were open, but his only words were "Oh, Jesus!"

After a while, I stood up and began making a count of the persons in the two rooms. Someone was missing. I finally sorted out who it was.

"Where's Howard Oliver?"

"He's probably still sleeping," several people said.

"Not at ten-thirty in the morning, with the pressure of not knowing about his wife out in Jonestown," I said. "I'm going to check."

Gordon Lindsay, the newsman, and I went to Howard's room on the seventh floor, where we found him face down on the floor. He had suffered a stroke. The tragedy of Jonestown was forgotten for a while; we had our own crisis to deal with. I opened Howard's medical alert bracelet to learn that he had had a stroke in 1969.

With much chasing and scurrying around, we managed to get a stretcher from the hotel and move him down to the lobby, where an ambulance was waiting outside. Howard was conscious, but one side of his mouth was obviously paralyzed. In spite of his condition and the concern of not knowing about his wife and two sons, he kept insisting, "I'll be all right, Bonnie. I'll be all right." We dashed toward the front doors. . . .

A familiar face caught the corner of my eye. I took a second look and nearly froze in my tracks. There in the lobby, watching all of us, was an entire delegation from Lamaha Gardens.

I pushed on toward the ambulance. The hotel manager was standing there, and I took the opportunity to vent my feelings. "What good does it do to have armed guards and dogs all around this place when a bunch of Peoples Temple members are standing right there in the lobby?" I fumed.

"I know, I know—we're going to take care of it right away," he said.

I jumped into the ambulance alongside Howard, and we were off for the hospital. Once he was under good medical care, I spent the next few hours trying to make arrangements for him to be flown back to San Francisco as soon as he was able. His condition seemed to stabilize.

It was late in the afternoon by the time I returned to the Pegasus and could think once again about my own future. Ambassador John Burke was still nowhere in sight, but one of his men had come and had convinced the rest of the relatives that our lives indeed were in danger. Tim Stoen had already arranged, through his brother in the States, for a United States Air Force C-130 Hercules to come to evacuate us late that evening.

I didn't want to go. None of my goals had been reached. I hadn't seen the people I came to see. And even though there had been a terrible tragedy at Port Kaituma, there were still people at Jonestown—I thought—who needed to be loved and supported. What was Marceline thinking right now? What had happened to the relatives we'd come for? I longed to be with them.

I tried calling my husband, but he was still at Sunday morning church; California was half a dozen hours behind Guyana time. Perhaps I should stay at the Pegasus anyway. Mickey Touchette was leaning the same way.

"You're fools," some of the others said. "What possible reason do you have for sticking around?"

I checked my wallet and realized that I couldn't afford to stay here very long. We had originally planned to end our visit today. I reluctantly headed upstairs to pack.

It was sometime during these hours that the mystery of Leo's refusal to allow me to use his plane to come to Jonestown was finally explained. I cannot reveal my source. I can only say that someone on the scene in Jonestown spoke with two of Jim's guards, who gave the chilling piece of information that Jim had ordered them to shoot me when I got off the plane. All of the relatives were to be shot, but I had the privilege of being lured by special invitation on Friday night to come early. Leo Ryan was probably not aware of Jim's order when he stopped me from coming. But he apparently sensed it in the air.

And by doing what he did he singlehandedly spared my life.

I was weak when I received the news. "Father" was my father no longer; he had become a madman. Apparently, in his mind, my presence in Jonestown would only have swelled the tide of defection. As his sons had already told me, I had come at the wrong time with the wrong people. So I needed to be killed immediately.

I gathered my things into my suitcase, while four or five Guyanese housemaids stood around crying, "Oh, missy," they wailed in their unique brand of English, "we don't know such a terrible group. Here in Guyana, we be good people. We would not allow this group if we knew."

"I'm sure that's true," I responded. "It's not your fault."

I was deeply touched when they wanted to pray with me. They led in a tender, emotional plea for comfort for the bereaved. And then I was on my way with the other relatives to the airport. A police motorcycle with lights flashing and siren screaming led the way for our two taxis and a van at high speeds over the twenty-six miles of dirt road. Guyana, formerly a British colony, retains left-hand driving, and as we chased through the city and past its outskirts, I was sure we were going to have an accident. At the airport we were whisked through a back entrance and into a VIP lounge shut off from the rest of the building. It was eight o'clock Sunday night.

Joe Hartman, an American official based at the airport, spent time with us and told us that helicopters flying over Jonestown had seen hundreds of people running into the jungle. He had been misinformed, we learned later. The C-130 was waiting outside, but there was a discussion with Guyanese officials about whether it could unload the communications equipment it had brought. As a result, we didn't leave at ten as promised. We waited.

By two in the morning, this night was beginning to feel the same as last night. Again we were holed up together in a room, tired, hungry, and desperate for information. All of a sudden—into the lounge walked Jim Cobb!

He looked like an animal. His black hair had not been combed, his clothes were mud-streaked, and his eyes were puffed into narrow slits. Mosquito bites covered his face and arms.

"Man, they were shooting people's brains out," he began to babble. "Leo's dead, and they were poisoning all these babies—they lined them up first. Some of the kids were kicking and screaming. . . ." His story came tumbling out in jumbled order, but his main point was unmistakable:

"Get on the plane and get out of here, because it's World War III in Jonestown. No one's going to be left alive."

He had been next to Greg Robinson, the young *San Francisco Examiner* photographer, on the airstrip, and they had fallen together when the shooting started. Jim thought Greg was just playing dead, and after a second, he grabbed Greg's shirt and yelled, "Don't lie there—run!" The newsman was too wounded to move.

Jim ducked under the plane and stood up on the other side—to find himself staring into the ends of two shotguns. Instantly he dove for the swamp; why they didn't shoot he could not explain. Once into the jungle, he climbed a tree to listen. Soon the roar from Jonestown told him that a full-scale holocaust was in session. Later that night a tiger had stalked underneath his perch. The mosquitoes were overwhelming, but he was determined to survive until morning, when he came out of the jungle and found two Guyanese soldiers.

He had talked to Odell Rhodes, another black man who escaped the mass suicide by volunteering to go for a stethoscope. Rhodes had hidden under a building for a while and then plunged into the jungle. Jim repeated his gruesome account of the death of the infants. He hadn't stayed long enough to see what happened to the adults, but the continued shouting and the gunfire left little doubt.

Jim had also learned that Jim Jones had dispatched two guards to hunt him down and kill him in the jungle. When they returned later, Jones asked excitedly, "Did you get Cobb? Did you get Cobb?"

"Yeah, we got him," they lied.

Jim had finally been flown by Guyanese police from Port Kaituma to the capital city and rushed over to join our homeward-bound group. We sat stunned as we listened to his tale of horror. It was becoming clearer all the time that the people we loved and had come to see were no longer alive.

It was the grace of God that allowed me to be forced to leave Guyana at that point. If I had actually seen Marceline's body, or Love Life's, I doubt that my mind could have withstood it without permanent damage. We moved silently into the bowels of the huge C-130 and strapped ourselves into the hammock-style seats that hung from the sides of the aircraft. Our luggage was loaded, and at about two-thirty we were ready to leave for San Juan, Puerto Rico.

A crew member came through to distribute ration boxes—a roast beef sandwich, a Milky Way candy bar, and some kind of orange drink made in Trinidad. I was too sick to eat. Instead, I sat staring at the others.

On the right side of the plane was elderly Nadyne Houston, tears running down her cheeks. Next came Grace Stoen, looking like a war orphan as she left the country without John-John for the second time. Next to her sat Clare Bouquette, and then Mickey Touchette, both with blank looks. At the end was Jim Cobb, still all psyched up.

On the left side of the plane beside me was Tim Stoen, bent over his ration box with his legs spread apart, munching on his sandwich and looking eighty years old. Wayne Pietila sat beside him, out of my line of sight.

Eight of us. We were leaving behind Howard Oliver in the hospital, Sherwin Harris to continue investigating the death of his children, and Steve Katsaris. Steve had already headed to Panama, where his son Anthony had been evacuated after taking bullets at the airstrip. Bev Oliver had been wounded in the feet at the same time. Carol Boyd was unhurt, but was returning home on another plane with the injured.

As the engines started warming up, a cloudlike gas began to emit from pipes high in the top of the aircraft. I watched incredulously as it became heavier and heavier, floating down to engulf us. All the Air Force crew members had disappeared. Soon I could not see to the other side of the plane.

"Tim, don't eat that sandwich," I cried. "It's contaminated." In my paranoia, the scene took on a bitter irony. *Just when we think we've finally gotten to safety, the United States Air Force is going to gas us to death to keep us from talking.* I waited for the suffocation to begin. *This is just how the Jews died. I wonder if they felt this peaceful.*

I took a deep breath and waited. Would I be dizzy or nauseous? Would my lungs collapse?

Suddenly a crew member walked past. I grabbed his coat.

"What's this gas?" I asked.

"Oh, it's nothing," he said. "Something to do with the air conditioning. It'll stop as soon as we're off the ground." The only reason I believed him was that he wasn't wearing a gas mask.

143

The sounds of flying soon put everyone to sleep except me. I wandered up to the cockpit after a while and stared at the rows upon rows of lights and dials. We were flying over the Caribbean, and there were only a few clouds below. I looked out at the lights of three oil tankers far beneath us. The moon was brightly illuminating the night, and in that moment, I wondered if it all hadn't been a bad dream. Perhaps I would awaken soon and find that none of the past week was true. If only . . .

We arrived in San Juan at six o'clock Monday morning, November 20, and Tim Stoen decided to stay there in order to find out more about John-John. The rest of us caught a little sleep in a hotel at the airport before boarding a commercial flight at 11:20 A.M. bound for New Orleans, Los Angeles, and finally San Francisco.

It was on the flight to New Orleans that I finally broke down completely. I had not had a normal meal since Saturday noon. My body was in extreme straits, and my mind would not stop thinking. What if Leo hadn't stopped me? What had Marceline done during the suicides? Did she go along with it, or did she resist? Was there any chance that she survived? Where was Jim? How was he planning to get out of all this?

I began to weep. I put on my sunglasses to cover up, but they did little good. Soon I broke into great, gasping sounds that I could not stop. The woman in the same row reached across a vacant seat to touch my arm, and at that, I went absolutely to pieces. She moved out to another seat to make room for Jim Cobb and Wayne Pietila, who came back to comfort me. Jim just held my hand, while Wayne let me sob into his shoulder. After about twenty minutes, I finally came under control. Wayne and I sat there quietly talking about how much we loved our spouses and how good it would be to see them again. It was a comforting thought.

I felt like a schmuck for falling apart, when others on the plane had probably lost blood relatives and were still maintaining their composure.

At New Orleans we got off the plane to buy a stack of newspapers, which confirmed Jim Cobb's report. Several hundred bodies had been found, most lying face down in the Jonestown pavilion or outside, having committed suicide. They believed Jim's teaching of reincarnation to the end, and when he promised, "We're going to meet in another place," they—at least some of them—had willingly drunk the cyanide Fla-Vour-Aid in order to get there. Surely the next incarnation would be better than facing the imagined tortures of the CIA or the Guyanese police.

We tore through the pages, looking for a list of names. There was none.

The group was quiet. "Do you think John's alive?" Grace Stoen kept asking, tears running down her face. No one could answer.

Soon we were back in the air, and at Los Angeles we were not allowed to leave the plane. But again, newspapers came on board, and when I saw the headline, I let out a groan.

CULT LEADER AND WIFE FOUND DEAD AMONG 300 BODIES

They were gone. She had stayed with him to the insane end. My mentor, the one woman I yearned most to see, for whose safe escape I would have given my own life . . . lay dead in the jungle. Her inscrutable husband lay dead as well, a victim of his own passions and theories. His paranoia had left him a shattered dictator, a broken god.

I sat staring out the window, thinking about the many ironies. He had railed incessantly against fascism, and in the end, he became the ultimate fascist. He promised to protect his people from concentration camps, and built one of his own. The Santayana quotation above his Jonestown throne, "Those who do not remember the past are condemned to repeat it," had been intended as a warning to blacks not to forget the lessons of Nazi Germany. The _ fate turned out to be worse than Auschwitz. And Jim's own demise turned out to be a shocking replay of Pharaoh Ikhnaton, who eventually forced Nefertiti to live alone while he consorted with mistresses in a separate castle, and seems to have died with them in a mass death by poisoning. His model city, Amarna, was left deserted and looted. . . .

We landed at San Francisco International Airport around six that evening and were whisked into a basement room where pairs of FBI agents were waiting at desks to interview each of us individually. After an hour of talking, we were asked if we wanted to confront the bank of cameras and reporters waiting outside. That was more than I could take at the moment. I waited in an FBI car while Grace Stoen, Jim Cobb, and some of the others talked to the press.

We were driven to the Federal Building for a change of cars and then on to the Human Freedom Center, a rambling two-story house in Berkeley. My husband had been notified by the FBI to meet me there, and of course he brought Stephan along. We fell into one another's arms; I hardly had the strength to kiss either of them.

"I'd never seen anything so pitiful in my life," Hank commented later. "You were like a rag doll. No expression, no energy. You slumped. All you wanted to do was go home."

I did manage to tell him that I was glad to be back and that I loved him. With that, we drove to pick up my car at Tim Stoen's house, and after the FBI had checked it out for bombs, we drove at long last toward Santa Cruz.

# sixteen FAREWELL TO LEO

THERE WAS YET ONE THING to be done. That was to say good-bye to the man who had saved my life.

The FBI agents, with whom I spent all Tuesday afternoon, were not excited about me showing my face on the streets of San Francisco. They had advised most of us to go into temporary hiding and think about moving, changing our phone numbers, and even our names. No one knew what the remnants of Peoples Temple might yet have in mind.

I didn't care. I had to go to Leo Ryan's funeral. On Wednesday morning I set out early to find All Souls' Church, where the mass would begin at eleven. It was raining. The church was on Walnut Street in San Francisco, I thought, but the closer I got, the worse the trip became. At one point I found myself headed down a one-way street the wrong way with three lanes of cars honking at me. I emerged without an accident, but barely.

Walnut Street turned out to be a tiny residential street with no Catholic church. I jumped out in the rain and asked a postman.

"You're in the wrong city, honey," he told me. "The funeral is at All Souls' Church on Walnut Street in *South* San Francisco. It's about thirty minutes from here back down the freeway."

I finally arrived at the church about 10:40, where a swarm of newspeople and a large crowd of Leo's friends and constituents were waiting outside. I pushed through to the guard at the front door and said, "I was with Leo in Guyana. Can you tell me how to get into the church?"

"You'll have to go around the side to where they're clearing people," he said.

I walked down a sloping hill and around to a lower-level entrance to the church. I approached a guard there, who sent me to one of the morticians, who brought me to a police or FBI officer. In my distraught state, I didn't notice which.

"Please, could you help me? My name is Bonnie Thielmann, and I was with Leo in Guyana. I came to the funeral to say good-bye and also to tell his family about the last hours I spent with him, and how much he loved them."

He wanted to see some identification.

I had cleaned out my purse of almost everything. I looked in vain for my passport, or an airline ticket; I couldn't even come up with my driver's license. A library card and a credit card were the best I could do.

"Lady, I'm sorry. There's no way I can believe you're who you say you are."

Suddenly I had an idea. "Call the FBI, sir—they interviewed me when I got back. They'll tell you who I am." I gave him the cards of three FBI agents I had talked to.

I stood there holding my umbrella and shaking in the rain while a call was made. In a few minutes, the word came back: "She's for real." He then sent me back to wait on the steps of the church for the rest of those who were to be seated first.

By that time the crowd outside had grown to more than eight hundred, and there was a lot of impatient pushing. Suddenly a line of dignitaries in black coats began marching in, and one of them bumped me, nearly knocking me over.

"I'm sorry," he said, reaching out to stabilize me. "Are you all right?"

"Yes," I said. "I was with Leo in Guyana, and they said I could come in, but I don't know when."

"Come with me," he said, taking my arm.

We started up the steps.

"Who are you?" I asked.

"My name's George Moscone."

My mind began to spin. I remembered back to the times at Peoples Temple when I had ushered George Moscone into services of lies and fraud. Suddenly here he was ushering me into a service of stark reality and truth.

The voice of the guard at the door brought me back to the present. "She can't come in."

Mayor Moscone simply said, "She's with me."

"OK," the guard replied, and we moved on into the narthex of the church. I was surrounded by congressmen and other dignitaries.

"Mr. Moscone," I said as we waited for seating, "I was an ex-temple member. I know people have criticized you

149

for your visits to Peoples Temple, but I want you to know that it really was a masquerade when you came. I'll gladly testify in your behalf if it will help people know that you were unaware of what Peoples Temple was really all about."

He patted my arm and said, "Thank you."

He was ushered to an appointed place on the right side of the church, while I was taken up to the second row on the left, where only two seats remained on the aisle. The rest of that row, as well as the first, was filled with congressmen and aides. I sat down, and soon another man in a black coat came along to complete the row.

The man on my left introduced himself, and when he learned who I was, proceeded to pass the word down the line. He was kind enough to lend me a handkerchief when I needed it.

Soon the service began. Joe Holsinger, the congressman's aide, gave the eulogy. I had not expected to find any comfort in this place; I had come rather to give what I could to the family once it was over. But then the priests began to read the Scriptures. Their choices were uncanny.

The first priest read the account of the last judgment from Matthew 25.

> *When the Son of man comes in his glory, and all the angels with him, then he will sit on his glorious throne. . . . Then the King will say to those at his right hand, "Come, O blessed of my Father, inherit the kingdom prepared for you from the foundation of the world; for I was hungry and you gave me food, I was thirsty and you gave me drink, I was a stranger and you welcomed me, I was naked and you clothed me, I was sick and you visited me, I was in prison and you came to me. . . . Truly, I say to you, as you did it to one of the least of these my brethren, you did it to me."*

It was the one Scripture that Jim Jones continued to harp on long after he had thrown his Bible away. He used it constantly to castigate the churches for their lack of practical action.

The priest pointed out that Leo Ryan had spent his life helping the least of the people, teaching in a tough school, spending time with the men in Folsom Prison, and finally going to Guyana when no one else would take it seriously. I thought about the fact that Leo didn't quote Matthew 25; he lived it instead.

The second priest read from John 15:13.

> *Greater love has no man than this, that a man lay down his life for his friends.*

Leo knew that Friday afternoon when we told him good-bye that he was going into something dangerous. The next day, he could have insisted on flying out first; he was the only one at that point whose life had been threatened, by Don Sly's knife. Leo could have made the defectors wait and perhaps been already inside the aircraft when the bullets began flying. Instead, he was out in the open, and he gave his life while others survived.

On the way out of the church, Jim Schollert stepped out from the seventh or eighth row to walk with me. "If Leo had to go," he said softly, "this is the way he would have wanted it. He's happier now."

I rode to the cemetery on one of the buses reserved for congressmen, thanks to having received a pass while sitting in their row. The flag over the casket was folded and given to Autumn Ryan, the congressman's mother. My emotions surged underneath throughout the graveside ritual, but I managed to stay in control.

My only other wish came true when, at a reception at the Hilton, I found Autumn Ryan and eventually was

151

given an opportunity to speak to the family, about thirty-five of them, in an upstairs suite. I told them how much Leo had talked about them during our time in Guyana.

"More than once he said, 'I love my children so much,' " I told them. " 'If it were my kids in Jonestown, I couldn't stand it.' That may not be much comfort to you now, but I wanted you to know that you were in his thoughts to the end."

The next day was Thanksgiving. I managed to sleep, in spite of nightmares, until ten o'clock that morning. It was an appropriate day to thank God for my safe return.

But at the same time, I was wounded and shaken by all I had been through. So many whom I loved were dead. "Oh, Lord," I prayed the next day, "I really need to understand. Why did it come out this way? What about those positive Scriptures you showed me the week before I went about the captives being set free? I was hoping that maybe nine-tenths of the people in Jonestown would 'return to their own land' as it said, and only one-tenth would be killed as it described in Zephaniah. Why did it come out just the opposite?"

My attention was drawn to Isaiah 55: 8-9.

> *This plan of mine is not what you would work out, neither are my thoughts the same as yours! For just as the heavens are higher than the earth, so are my ways higher than yours, and my thoughts than yours.*

I was left to play the role of God's fool, to admit that regardless of my intelligence, he has more, and that he could use the tragedy of Peoples Temple to speak to us all about the meaning of life and death, truth and error. And in that, I must rest.

# epilogue WHAT WE MUST DO

THE LESSONS OF JONESTOWN will be pondered for a long time. I would like to comment regarding three of them.

First of all, we must close the loopholes in our legal code that allow dangerous groups to call themselves religious and thereby avoid public scrutiny. I am not an attorney or a judicial scholar, but I believe a way must be found to permit *unannounced* observation of such groups by government officials. Once they know a visitor is coming, the whole charade begins, and nothing is seen as it really is. Without endangering other rights, we must change our laws in order to find out what people such as Jim Jones are up to.

# THE BROKEN GOD

When I returned from Guyana, I asked FBI agents why they hadn't done anything about Jim Jones until now. Their answer was simple: "Peoples Temple was a church. Our hands were tied."

Secondly, we must support groups that sensitively, tenderly, lovingly know how to deprogram cult defectors. The Human Freedom Center, 302 Regent Street, Berkeley, California 94705, is one such group run by Al and Jeannie Mills, former members of Peoples Temple. There are other such groups who are willing to listen and to love broken human wreckage, and still more are needed.

Thirdly, Christians must get their act together in terms of practical caring and loving. We must start doing the things Jesus told us to do. We must come to terms with racism in our midst. We must obey such commands as Isaiah 58:7-8:

> *I want you to share your food with the hungry and bring right into your own homes those who are helpless, poor and destitute. Clothe those who are cold and don't hide from relatives who need your help. If you do these things, God will shed his own glorious light upon you. He will heal you; your godliness will lead you forward, and goodness will be a shield before you, and the glory of the Lord will protect you from behind.*

If we were doing that, cults such as Peoples Temple would lose their magnetism. Their suction power is in direct proportion to the church's lack of concern and love.

With initiatives such as these, the horror of the cult of death can be prevented from happening again. That is my prayer.

154